Classic Restaurants

of

FORT WAYNE

·········· KEITH ELCHERT AND LAURA WESTON

AMERICAN PALATE

Published by American Palate
A Division of The History Press
Charleston, SC
www.historypress.com

Front Cover (clockwise from top left): Zesto's (Authors' collection), the Hobby House (*News-Sentinel*), Jack & Johnny's (Authors' collection), Coney Island (*News-Sentinel*) and Gardner's (Randy Harter).
Back Cover (from left to right): Pagoda Inn (Randy Harter) and Zoli's (*News-Sentinel*).

First published 2019

Manufactured in the United States

ISBN 9781625859549

Library of Congress Control Number: 2018966324

Notice: The information in this book is true and complete to the best of our knowledge. It is offered without guarantee on the part of the author or The History Press. The author and The History Press disclaim all liability in connection with the use of this book.

Contents

Acknowledgements   5
Introduction   7

1. Neighborhood Hangouts   9
2. Fun Food (Burgers, Ice Cream and More)   33
3. A Little More Upscale   52
4. Ethnic Restaurants   66
5. Fondly Remembered   83

Selected Bibliography   105
Index   107
About the Authors   111

Acknowledgements

We would like to thank the following people for their assistance, whether it was with brainstorming, with photographs or with information: Bob Baker; Daniel Baker; John Beatty, of the Allen County Public Library; Lauren Caggiano; Walter Font, at the History Center; Jeff Harvey; Jill McDevitt and Andrea Kern, of ARCH; Brad Saleik; John Stein and Brian Tombaugh.

As we mention in our introduction, the resources of the *Fort Wayne News-Sentinel* were invaluable in the creation of this work. We are immensely grateful to former editor Kerry Hubartt for allowing us access and to all the journalists whose work preceded ours.

Finally, we owe a special debt of gratitude to Randy Harter, who blazed a path for us in so many ways and was also gracious enough to keep us on our own path.

Introduction

You know how nostalgic Fort Wayne folks can get about food, especially when the eatery was downtown in the 1940s, '50s or '60s. Just mention Gardner's or Lenkendofer's or Manochio's or the Blue Moo, and most local old-timers will shake their heads wistfully and raise their eyes toward heaven. "Best (burgers/ nuts/popcorn/milkshakes) ever," they'll say. "I remember going there after (high school/shopping/work/the war). Those were happy times."
—*Carol Tannehill*
Fort Wayne News-Sentinel
March 29, 2002

Fort Wayne is known as the City of Churches, for reasons that seem obvious. It is also known as the Summit City, for being situated atop the highest land in northeast Indiana. It is even known as the City that Saved Itself, after its efforts to combat a spring 1982 flood drew the attention—not to mention the assistance in stacking sandbags—of President Ronald Reagan.

Fort Wayne also is known as a city of restaurants. And the early twenty-first century has seen a renaissance; intriguing new eateries such as Tolon, the Proximo and the Friendly Fox are opening throughout the city with regularity. Well-loved, long-standing favorites remain as well, characterized by what Carol Tannehill said of Powers Hamburgers in 2006: "comforting continuity."

Speaking of Tannehill, you will see the name of the longtime *News-Sentinel* restaurant reviewer pop up frequently throughout these pages. Also here are book coauthor Laura Weston, another former reviewer for the *News-Sentinel*, and her predecessor, Cindy Larson. We owe special thanks to the newspaper and its writers. Editor Kerry Hubartt generously allowed us access to the *News-Sentinel* archives, which made this a much more complete book in both words and photographs. The citations to the dozens of articles we combed would fill a book all on their own.

We are under no illusion, however, that our list is complete, or even completely representative of the Fort Wayne food experience. How do you capture, for instance, Three Rivers Festival's Junk Food Alley for someone who has never experienced it firsthand? Other aspects of Fort Wayne food lore, whether it be Seyfert's potato chips, the Bun bar or the Pizza Hut empire of Dick Freeland, have to settle for their mention here. We did, however, venture out into the rest of Allen County to include a few of the better-known eateries there.

Nor do we make any claim that these words fully capture the experience of late nineteenth-century and much of twentieth-century Fort Wayne. If there is one thing we have learned as we complete our third book taking a look at long-ago places, it's that too many stories have already been lost to time. Our most fervent hope is that we have captured as many as possible before they all disappear.

So, if find yourself saying, "I can't believe they left out (insert omission here)," that is okay. We hope you will let us know; it will simply make future printings of the book that much more inclusive. We enjoy learning from fellow lovers of history—and food.

1
Neighborhood Hangouts

THE ACME

1105 East State Boulevard

The Acme has been a neighborhood fixture on Fort Wayne's near-northeast side for going on eight decades. In fact, its motto is "Where neighbors meet."

Nicholas Cozmas, a native of Macedonia, bought the bar in 1941. In the late 1970s, the Acme passed into the hands of Cozmas's son-in-law Mike Tapp, who once explained how the slogan captures "the image we want. We don't have anything fancy in wine sauce or stuff like that," he said, "just good food." The Acme was also known as a destination for that Indiana staple—the breaded tenderloin. Tapp received many out-of-town requests for the Hoosier delicacy; those who asked were happy to settle for him shipping them a frozen version.

A 1985 *News-Sentinel* story detailed one of the more unusual occurrences at the Acme: It "may be the only area tavern that ever caught a bank robber.... One day (the article makes no mention of when), a customer ran in to say a nearby bank had been robbed. The suspect made the mistake of trying to hide in the Acme's dumpster. No problem. In the back room was Fred Beck, a Fort Wayne policeman. He walked out the back door, reached in and arrested him."

An Acme meeting room was the location for another out-of-the-ordinary occurrence; it hosted an Alcoholics Anonymous meeting every Friday afternoon for more than ten years. "What's a more natural place to have a meeting than at a bar?" one group member was quoted as saying. "If you can stay sober at the bar, you can stay sober during the rest of the day."

The Acme went dark for a time in the early 2000s; ownership cited the city's newly enacted smoking ban as a reason. Jeff and Amy Parrish took up the challenge and reopened the Acme in February 2010. Among their innovations is "tap takeovers," where a local microbrewery is featured at the Acme's 26 taps for an evening.

The tavern's decorations are eclectic. Large paintings of Fort Wayne's Parkview Field and New York's Yankee Stadium (the old one) dominate a wall

The Acme has been a place "where neighbors meet" on East State Boulevard for more than seventy years. *Authors' collection.*

in the bar and dining room, respectively. (An advertisement for the Acme has been painted into each scene.) Vintage signs for Centlivre and Berghoff beers pay tribute to the city's brewing history. A checkerboard black-and-white floor, vinyl-padded booths and an old jukebox add a diner vibe.

BILLY'S DOWNTOWN ZULU

18000 LINCOLN HIGHWAY EAST, ZULU

"Downtown Zulu" is meant to be taken ironically—Billy's pretty much *is* Downtown Zulu. But the name is very much in keeping with the spirit of an eastern Allen County bar/restaurant, where miniature statues of the Blues Brothers greet you at the entrance.

Billy's has been serving winning bar food, with an emphasis on Mexican, since 1982. (The Haystack Inn preceded Billy's on the site.) Mike Adams, along with his wife, Lorie, took ownership of the restaurant in 2012. Mike is a friend of previous owner Bob Carney.

Billy's is a landmark to look for on your drive through eastern Allen County's "downtown Zulu." *Courtesy News-Sentinel.*

"My wife and I had many, many, many fun experiences (at Billy's)," Mike says. "We decided we didn't want to see it go down the tubes."

The Adamses decided not to mess with a winning formula, though Mike says the restaurant (still named after the 1982 owner Billy Nessman) was in "dire, dire need of upgrading." The inside was completely remodeled, though Jake and Elwood Blues retain their places of honor. The plaid upholstery for the seats stayed, too. Posters of college mascots let you know you are in the heart of Big Ten country. And recipes that had been set aside are in use again.

"We tried to recapture all that for customers who remember Billy's from what it was when it started," Mike says. He adds that he can tell he is onto something by the number of leftover containers he is going through. "The servings are plentiful, and the recipes are good," he says.

BOB'S RESTAURANT

22031 MAIN STREET, WOODBURN

Pie is why many people make the stop east of Fort Wayne at Bob's. "Life's short. Eat pie" is the motto of this destination diner.

As described in Laura Weston-Elchert's 2015 review: "Bob's is a hometown hangout, where everyone seems to know each other.

In Woodburn, Bob's Restaurant is the place to go for daily food specials and a great selection of pies—if you arrive early enough. *Authors' collection.*

Conversation flowed freely not only at tables, but also between them....(B)y the end of the meal, we felt like locals."

Pinwheels predominate among the diner's decor. The walls are also liberally adorned with newspaper clippings tracing the career of Woodburn native Lloy Ball, a college and Olympic gold medal–winning volleyball standout who went to school at nearby IPFW (Indiana University–Purdue University Fort Wayne).

A pie board lists the day's choices. Diners have to keep a close eye on the board, though, as selections are summarily erased as patrons gobble them up.

DASH-IN CAFÉ

814 SOUTH CALHOUN STREET

"Meet me at the Dash" has been an invitation for downtown diners for nearly twenty years. *Authors' collection.*

Neil Colchin (a former United Parcel Service employee) and Lynn Podzielinski realized their dream of a West Coast–style coffeehouse in downtown Fort Wayne in 1994. Their vision was of a place where you could get bagels, fresh fruit and sandwiches while enjoying conversation and local artwork.

Enough fans shared the vision that within two years, the Dash-In moved across the street into a more spacious location. The coffeehouse went from eight hundred square feet to more than three thousand; the space was defined by its exposed brick walls and high ceilings.

The Dash-In has evolved through the years; it now boasts brews alongside coffee. "Life is short, drink good beer" reads the slogan at the top of the Dash-In website. "We serve a large selection of craft beer, 23 rotating taps and over 50 craft beers in the bottle," it adds. And as for the food: "We focus on the smallest of details when we prepare our soups from scratch, slow-roast our pulled pork, and construct our desserts and baked goods."

THE GREEN FROG

820 SPRING STREET

The name is a nod to the ugly green paint obtained on the cheap when the neighborhood tavern needed a touchup in the early 1940s ("and it was also where you could get your hops," said owner and Fort Wayne first lady Cindy Henry). The name and the outer color scheme have stayed ever since.

Cindy Henry is the most recent in a female ownership line that extends back to the tavern's 1935 beginnings. At the time Alice Morton opened her establishment, women were not even allowed to sit at the bar.

The Green Frog prides itself as a neighborhood tavern. Its website touts the tavern as "the 'Cheers!' of Fort Wayne"—an important distinction in the hometown of *Cheers* costar Shelley Long. It is part of a German Catholic neighborhood anchored by Most Precious Blood Catholic Church. The Green Frog also prides itself on its consistency. "Every (person) that hasn't

Left: Denny and Teena Durnell's namesake tavern, at 2502 Broadway Street, has operated since 1950 in a building converted from an Eckrich meatpacking plant. In a review from 2009, the *News-Sentinel*'s Cindy Larson called the neighborhood tavern a "cozy-looking little pub" featuring "a cute back room with a fireplace." *Authors' collection.*

Right: The Green Frog is a restaurant popular among residents of the neighborhood that surrounds Most Precious Blood Catholic Church. But the rest of the city has learned the secret. *Authors' collection.*

been in here for a long time comes in and says that it hasn't changed a bit," Henry told a newspaper interviewer in 2002.

Henry ceded control of the Green Frog to Matt Billings in 2016 but returned in 2019; patrons were notified courtesy of a big "Cindy's back" banner out front. And in case you are wondering, frogs' legs are served at the Green Frog; they are available daily and as the Thursday night special.

HALL'S

BLUFFTON ROAD DRIVE-IN, 1502 BLUFFTON ROAD

Also owned by the Hall family:
Commissary Restaurant, 216 Highway 930 West, New Haven
The Deck, 306 East Superior Street
The Factory, 5811 Coldwater Road
Food Factory Express, 1504 Bluffton Road
The Gas House, 305 East Superior Street
Guest House Bar & Grill, 1313 West Washington Center Road
Lima Road Drive-In, 4416 Lima Road
State Street Prime Rib, 2005 East State Boulevard
Takaoka of Japan, 305 East Superior Street
Tap Haus, 216 Highway 930 West, New Haven
The Tavern, 5745 Coventry Lane
Triangle Park, 3010 Trier Road

On the day after Thanksgiving in 1946, Don Hall started a chain that has come to dominate the city's culinary landscape.

The Hall family operated a meat market on South Calhoun Street. But as supermarkets became more common in the post–World War II era, Don Hall worried increasingly about his business's long-term prospects. One day while making his delivery rounds, he took note of a plot of undeveloped land that would become the launching spot for his vision. Hall's Drive-In opened at Quimby Village; that location remains open today. The restaurant originally was a dining room only; the drive-up window and carhops were added after the first three years.

Don's son Bud managed the drive-in, which has been lauded by *News-Sentinel* columnist Kevin Leininger as having "epitomized Fort Wayne's youth culture in the post–World War II era." In a 1983 interview,

Top: The curved facade of Hall's original Bluffton Road restaurant hints at its onetime— and future—existence as a drive-in restaurant. The building was enclosed in 1969. *Authors' collection.*

Bottom, left: Fort Wayne brewing pioneer Charles L. Centlivre stands watch over diners on the deck at the downtown Hall's Gas House. *Authors' collection.*

Bottom, right: A mailbox from the Van Orman Hotel, which sat at Berry and Harrison Streets, is one of the reclaimed Fort Wayne artifacts on display at Hall's Gas House location. *Authors' collection.*

Bud Hall recalled the drive-in as a popular lower-cost alternative for family dining. "Back then, there weren't many restaurants except for the formal, higher-priced supper clubs," he said. "Drive-ins were priced so that you could take the kids out." That era, which included the expansion of the menu to include such then-exotic curbside entrees as barbecue sandwiches and beef platters, lasted until 1969, when the drive-in area was enclosed. (The entire restaurant had been rebuilt and enlarged following a 1962 fire.)

Hall's Hollywood Drive-In still offers the carhop experience with space for nineteen cars at the restaurant at 4416 Lima Road. But once again proving that everything old is new again, Hall's announced in July 2017 that drive-in service would return to the Bluffton Road location. About fifty dining room seats will be sacrificed to restore a half-dozen of what was once a total of thirty-eight drive-in spots. "This is overdue, and I'm confident it will be well-received," said Jeff Hall (Bud's brother). "This will be romantic, a reminder of a simpler time." The hope is to attract a younger demographic as well as those hungry for nostalgia. Added Bud Hall: "We've been (on Bluffton Road) through the good and bad times, even when nobody was here. But this (place) is our roots. If you sit still long enough, things will come back past you."

In 1957, Hall's Gas House, on Superior Street, became the second restaurant in the chain that grew to include twelve (plus one in Indianapolis) and a hotel. The Gas House building is also home to Takaoka of Japan (1978), a steakhouse named in honor of one of Fort Wayne's several sister cities. (The others are Gera, Germany; Plock, Poland; and Taizhou, China.)

A commissary location in New Haven supplies ingredients, including horseradish sauce, blue cheese dressing and pulled pork for all the Hall's locations.

When Don Hall died in 1972, the business passed into the hands of his children. The grocery stores he sold all those years ago had been purchased by Carlyle Pio. The last of three Pio's Markets remains in operation today at 1225 East State Boulevard, next to the former Rib Room and Nick's Martini Bar.

In 2003, Hall's Gas House decided to take advantage of its location overlooking the St. Marys River to add a deck. That deck's popularity in the years since has been among the catalysts in Fort Wayne's push for a San Antonio–style riverfront development. "We believed in downtown when nothing was happening downtown," Bud Hall said. And overlooking that deck is a tribute to one of Fort Wayne's brewing pioneers. Perched atop the northeast corner of the Gas House is a sculpture of Charles L.

Centlivre. The statue was commissioned in 1911 by Centlivre employees in memory of the brewery's founder. Centlivre's foot rests atop a keg of beer as he gazes up Spy Run Avenue toward the site of his former business and nearby Centlivre Park.

Extensive renovations took place at the Gas House in 2008, when the restaurant was shut down for three months as NIPSCO (Northern Indiana Public Service Company) dealt with 2.4 million gallons of coal tar and contaminants left underneath the building from the days the site was an actual gas plant. Other Fort Wayne artifacts have assumed a place in the Gas House decor, including a mail drop box from the Van Orman Hotel and a sculpture of a lion's head that adorned the Barr Street Market in front of the 1910 city hall.

In 2008, Bud Hall summed up his family's success thusly: "We understand the Fort Wayne market, and offer a good deal for the money." And the life of Bud's brother Sam Hall was the embodiment of the family philosophy. When he died on April 8, 2017, he was cooking breakfast for customers at Hall's New Haven restaurant. Sam had returned to the grill after the 2012 passing of his wife, Dede, a former Fort Wayne city councilwoman. Don Connett, general manager of Hall's Triangle Park restaurant, was Sam's friend of 40 years. "He was a very simple guy," Connett said. "In the restaurant business where you could have anything, he'd have a cheeseburger."

In 2018, Hall's announced plans to expand its presence along Fort Wayne's revitalized riverfront. A structure known as the Cambray Building had been slated for demolition to advance riverfront development. Bud Hall purchased and moved the 36-by-100-foot, 500-ton structure with the intent of converting the building into a nightspot. "With the building's architecture, I wanted to save it even though I didn't know what I would do with it," Hall told an interviewer. The building was moved to its permanent location on February 5, 2019.

An updated Cambray Building will only add to the Hall's presence in the middle of the riverfront revival. In addition to the Gas House, which also sits on the south bank of the St. Marys River, Bud Hall is also responsible for the 1976 restoration of the Cass Street Depot on the river's north bank.

HENRY'S RESTAURANT

536 West Main Street

If the Trolley Bar was the journalists' hangout of an earlier age, Henry's (located just to the east of the Fort Wayne Newspapers building) has long since assumed the title. "Meet me at Henry's" has been a slogan for reporters and plenty of others since this downtown tavern's 1959 opening. Writer Lou Henry (no relation) says of the Henry's experience:

> *Henry's is the kind of establishment in which you look forward to having a drink. It's quiet and dark, and you are almost guaranteed to see someone you know. It has a classic, warm, library feel to it. I say library because there are books placed on shelves around the bar, along with antique instruments and local artwork. You get a taste of Fort Wayne's flavor to go along with the flavor of your dinner.*

Henry's, a Main Street mainstay, has added outdoor dining to complement the seating in its warmly inviting interior. *Authors' collection.*

JACK & JOHNNY'S

1234 NORTH WELLS STREET

The intersection of Wells and High Streets soon will see customers again; Christina Mills and Jeff Witcher are renovating Jack & Johnny's restaurant. *Authors' collection.*

Jack & Johnny's last dimmed its signature lantern in 2008. Since then, regulars—up to one hundred—have been meeting annually at other restaurants for a reunion. That is a lot of loyalty for a place that claimed "the customer is never right." And soon, they will be able to return to their beloved original.

The husband-and-wife team of Christina Mills and Jeff Witcher announced plans in May 2017 to reopen under the Jack & Johnny's name. They envision a restaurant that eventually will include a rooftop garden in addition to second-floor seating (once a spiral staircase is replaced). And they plan to draw on both Mills's two decades of bartending and Witcher's experience as a cook. Of the decor, Mills told an interviewer: "We want to leave the nostalgia and upgrade what's needed." The nostalgia will include about a dozen menu favorites, including the chisam sandwich—chicken, Swiss cheese and ham.

Jack Humbrecht and Johnny Pence, in conjunction with their wives (Johnny's wife was Jack's sister), bought what had been the Wells Street Tap in 1945. A *News-Sentinel* story reported: "Mills and Witcher have found items from other former lives of the building…soda flavorings and pharmacy bottles that show the bar likely once was where customers drank sodas, and a 1937 liquor license for the Wells Lunch."

The tavern originally operated next door, where a parking lot is now located. Humbrecht and Pence moved it in 1962 when a storefront became available. A second generation of cousins, Greg Humbrecht and Greg Pence, ran Jack & Johnny's until health complications forced them to close the restaurant.

Loyalty proved to be a quality of customers and employees alike. Jack & Johnny's once boasted a group of five workers with a combined two hundred years of service. At another time, three generations of women from the same family worked there simultaneously.

"I've owned it 64 years," Jack Humbrecht said in 2010. "My partner and I, we ran the place for 45 years and never had an argument. He had to be the nicest guy in the world to put up with me."

Before Mills and Witcher took over, the building last served as local headquarters for the 2016 Bernie Sanders presidential campaign.

KLEMM'S CANDLELIGHT CAFÉ

1207 EAST STATE STREET

After Herman Handy's original Candlelight Café closed in the early 1990s, restaurateur Mike Klemm decided to open a second location (his original is at 1429 North Wells Street). Klemm even brought back retired cook Lucille Chester. The Candlelight's counter and table seating can accommodate up to eighty patrons; they stop in for the traditional breakfast and lunch offerings. Pan-fried chicken is a particular specialty.

LAYCOFF'S BAR & GRILL

530 NORTH CLINTON STREET

Thanks to a $20,000 city façade grant, the exterior of Laycoff's received a face-lift in 2016. Inside, the food remains as good as it ever was.

Lazar and Alexandria Laycoff, Macedonian immigrants, opened their own place in 1956 after nearly two decades as partners with Thomas Lazoff in the L&L Tavern on Lafayette Street. Son Cyril and his wife, Barbara, also took to the family business, with the couple's daughters sometimes sleeping in a booth until Laycoff's closed at 3:00 a.m.

From 1979 to 1994, the Laycoff family operated a second location at Pine Valley in northwest Fort Wayne.

In 1998, the Laycoff family decided to explore life away from the restaurant business. "Some people have been coming in here for years," reminisced Angie Laycoff-Richards. "We see them pull into the parking lot, and we have their drink waiting for them when they walk in."

Laycoff's is once again looking good along North Clinton Street. Owner Jimmy Sullivan says the 2016 face-lift "has helped out a bunch." *Authors' collection.*

Jimmy Sullivan acquired the tavern and opted to keep the name in a move driven by equal parts business sense and nostalgia. Sullivan said he looked at more than a dozen properties in his effort to buy into the restaurant business. He settled on Laycoff's in part because "I'd come in as a kid" with his grandfather.

That grandfather was Jimmy D'Angelo, a member of one of Fort Wayne's first families of restaurants. So as Sullivan thought of tweaking Laycoff's menu, he wisely reached back to his family's culinary roots. That is evident from the first bite of the salad, which will taste familiar to anyone who has ever had a salad at one of Fort Wayne's Casa restaurants.

Sullivan reports that his experience with loyal clientele has been similar to that of the founding family. "We have people who come in six days a week," he says. "We know their drinks. We know their lives. They're our friends; we go out with them."

"If you're gonna be in this business," Sullivan adds, "you really gotta enjoy people."

NINE MILE RESTAURANT
13398 U.S. 27

This restaurant derived its name from its location; it was nine miles from the Allen County Courthouse at the time of its opening. That was in 1837. (Nine Mile is in the running for the title of the oldest bar in Indiana.)

John Karn was the original tavern owner; he sold out to John Holmes thirteen years later. Holmes added an Inn and gave the place the name it has had ever since. The roofline of that 1850 addition remains visible above other additions that have been built around it.

"The site became one of the most important gathering places in the southern part of the county—a place where (stagecoach) travelers spent the night and where pioneers met to exchange news over a pint," Allen County Public Library genealogist John D. Beatty told an interviewer. (In more modern times, Nine Mile would be the site of a Phillips 66 gas station in addition to the tavern.)

Beatty said his wife is a native of Marion Township, where Nine Mile is located. "(We) think she probably had an ancestor that came here 100 years ago!" he said.

Of the present-day Nine Mile, *News-Sentinel* restaurant reviewer Cindy Larson observed: "It does feel like a roadhouse, as it's kind of out in the middle of nowhere. Its lighted sign is a welcome beacon on a dark, cold night."

The Greek Revival style of the original 1830s building remains apparent in this 1930s photograph of the Nine Mile Restaurant. *Courtesy Allen County Public Library.*

"Just about every time we go," she added, "we see neighbors or friends."

Among the specialty items on the Nine Mile menu are fried pickle spears and fried chicken gizzards. And Larson noted that the menu "is varied and should satisfy the meat-and-potato lover, those who prefer fish or seafood, and the health-conscious who gravitate toward salads. Barbecue ribs and Wednesday's Mexican nights are particularly popular draws."

OLDE TOWNE DINER

14515 LEO ROAD, LEO-CEDARVILLE

You can probably find something you will enjoy in a restaurant that greets you with a pie case as soon as you walk in the front door. And Olde Towne's diner fare more than lives up to the promise.

"We cook everything from scratch," restaurant veteran and diner co-owner Peg Funk said on opening in 2007. The mission statement Funk and Dan Kneubuhler share on their menu fleshes out that philosophy. "It is a great pleasure to welcome you and your family to our diner," they write. "It is our passion to serve you quality, delicious food, with great service at a fair price. We want you to experience some old-fashioned goodness that everyone needs a little of in this fast paced world." That menu features sandwiches (available as baskets and platters as well), soups, salads and those desserts.

Inside the Olde Towne Diner's rather modest-looking exterior waits a food and atmosphere experience that will transport you back to the 1950s—whether you lived through them or not. *Authors' collection.*

Reviewer Carol Tannehill christened the décor as "Mayberry meets Happy Days":

> *The restaurant is part 1950s drive-in and part old-timey ice cream parlor. It's sleek yet cozy. It's chrome paired with painted wood. It's lustrous table tops teamed with candy-stripe awnings.*

Framed black-and-white photographs of James Dean, Elvis and Marilyn in her best *Seven Year Itch* pose add authenticity to the ambience. New ownership has made the sound decision to keep things pretty much as they have been.

RACK & HELEN'S

525 BROADWAY STREET, NEW HAVEN

The name of this tavern comes from founders Erwin "Rack" and Helen Rekeweg. The husband-and-wife team opened the tavern in downtown New Haven in 1972. A year later, John "Pat" Anderson partnered with the Rekewegs. After some time away from ownership, Anderson and his wife, Myra, decided in 2000 to repurchase Rack's. These days, son Wes has joined them in the ownership group.

Upon reacquisition, the Andersons decided Rack's needed a greater emphasis on food. As their website tells the tale: "Great food, great service, and an inviting friendly environment propelled Rack's into a busy hangout for New Haven's locals and others from surrounding communities."

Pat Anderson is the patriarch of the two-generation management team at Rack & Helen's in Downtown New Haven. *Courtesy News-Sentinel.*

A kitchen that could only comfortably accommodate two employees soon became overtaxed. "Dishes were washed by hand and busy days meant serving 30–40 lunches." Two expansions— with the more intensive one in 2008—have resulted in a tavern that can seat 200 (up from 85), plus another 140 in a banquet room. Rack & Helen's also boasts a state-of-the-art kitchen for its dine-in and catering operations.

As for the food, it is everything you would expect from a bar—and then some. Half-pound burgers share menu space with blackened tilapia and lemon pepper shrimp scampi. And the numerous barbecue entrees (ribs, pulled pork, etc.) come with a selection of Rack's signature sauces: Sweet BBQ, Hot BBQ, Carolina BBQ, Rack's Buffalo, Cherry Bourbon BBQ and Cajun Butter.

Trivia, karaoke and occasional live performers offer accompaniment to the dining and imbibing experience. And there is more, according to an impressed reviewer from 2010. "What used to be a typical small-town bar (except for the upside-down sign) is now a hip sports bar," wrote Cindy Larson. "The attractive brick exterior complements the upgrades to New Haven's street scape. And the interior is surely a sports spectator's dream. From my seat I could see seven TVs."

In 2017, the Lodge at Coyote Creek, on Fort Wayne's Hillegas Road, received a makeover, becoming Rack & Helen's Social House. The partnership between the restaurants focused on made-from-scratch ingredients, including ketchup, mustard, pickles, barbecue sauce, hush puppies and Italian sausage.

REDWOOD INN

1432 WEST MAIN STREET

Mark Nei bought the Redwood in 2015. It remains the neighborhood place of his youth (he grew up along Main Street)—only cleaner.

Nei's first task after assuming ownership was a thorough going-over of the interior. Years of residue were wiped off the walls and even the lightbulbs. But there were minimal changes to the menu. Fans can still get the pizzas, homemade Boston clam chowder, sausage rolls and Greek salad for which the Redwood is known.

The most noticeable change may be on the outside. Nei added an outdoor seating area, accented by a well-manicured grassy area and sculptures, to the east of building.

The Redwood location has been home to a restaurant as far back as 1928. The site has also been home to a radio repair shop.

For at least one patron, the pre-renovation Redwood evoked nothing so much as *The Godfather* movies.

News-Sentinel columnist Lou Henry wrote:

We were tucked in the back of the small "Little Italy"–type bar. The restaurant felt like it was missing an accordion player and some old Italian man crooning for the ladies. The tables had the standard red-and-white tablecloths, and the atmosphere was smoky and smelled of baking dough and tomato sauce. It felt like I was in an old movie, and my friends and I were gangsters talking about…"making offers that they can't refuse."

The addition of a patio and sculpture garden have enhanced the appeal of the Redwood Inn, where dishes as diverse as Greek salad, clam chowder and pizza all come highly recommended. *Authors' collection.*

In researching a presentation on Fort Wayne bars, historian David B. Lupke managed to trace the Redwood's full lineage, calling it "a strong candidate for second oldest continuously operating bar in Fort Wayne."

The Redwood began its life in 1893. It was known at various times as the Hammerle Tavern, the Evelyn Robbins Restaurant, and the Home Lunch, which was a café that served alcohol. During Prohibition, liquor was served in coffee or in coffee cups and the Home Lunch was open twenty-four hours a day, seven days a week. In 1955, Joe Bankert bought the tavern and renamed it Joe's Tap Tavern and the Lug A Jug Liquor Store. Wes Stewart bought the tavern in 1962 and renamed it the Redwood Inn. Dan and Jeanne Bixby bought the tavern in 1977, and in September 2014, Mark Nei became the latest owner.

RICHARDS

717 WEST WASHINGTON CENTER ROAD

"Serve hot food hot and cold food cold! It seems pretty simple to me." From that basic philosophy arose a culinary and entertainment empire.

By the time he founded Richards in 1967, the speaker of those words, Don Strong, was already a successful restaurateur. He started with a downtown Bluffton diner called Snug. Then with the assistance of his mother, Gladys (who oversaw the baking), plus his wife, Mona Jean, and other family members, Strong opened the much larger Embers restaurant in Portland.

The company website expounds on the founder's vision:

> *Over the years Richards has built new restaurants, renovated exiting restaurants and redesigned interior layouts several times, but the basic Company philosophy has remained the same—provide Good Food at Reasonable Prices and do it quickly in a Friendly Atmosphere. There's nothing fancy here, just basic, down home goodness.*

Longtime Fort Wayne resident and *News-Sentinel* restaurant critic Carol Tannehill had a different take. "The Richards I remember (the now-closed one on Paulding Road)," she wrote in 2004, "was like the resident lounge in the nursing home where I used to visit an aging relative in the 1970s. The décor was pastel Country Primitive and, everywhere you looked, there were old people eating and smoking." But after her 2004 visit, Tannehill reported that "both my attitude and Richards have undergone major changes. I've decided to go to Richards regularly. You're never too young for affordable breakfasts, mile-high cream pie and to-die-for cinnamon rolls."

In 1975, Strong bought a farm in the town of Bryant in Jay County. He named it Bearcreek and turned it into a place that could be enjoyed by his family, his employees and, eventually, the public. Bearcreek Farm closed in 2012, but it lives on through the Bearcreek Memories Dinner Theater in nearby Celina, Ohio. Among the entertainers on the schedule: the Lettermen, the Van-Dells and Brenda Lee.

And though only one Fort Wayne Richards location remains, Auburn, Bluffton, Columbia City, Decatur, Kokomo, Muncie, New Haven, Portland and Warsaw are also home to Richards restaurants. Richards also runs Ranch House restaurants in Huntington and Kendallville.

TRION TAVERN

503 BROADWAY STREET, NEW HAVEN

What could be more central to a downtown than a tavern at the intersection of Main and Broadway Streets? How about a tavern that has managed to turn New Haven into Brew Haven once every year?

Trion owner Greg Jacquay is the force behind the event that has drawn brewers and craft beer seekers every June since 2011. Brew Haven was an extension of Jacquay's vision of his tavern. As explained in a 2013 profile:

> Beer aficionados made the Trion one of Allen County's premier destinations even before (craft beer) was trendy. Beginning with fewer than ten little-known brews, the Trion today offers fifty-eight different beers of all hues and flavors, and the numerous tap handles that move from the wall to the bar depending on what's available offer proof that the beer lineup is constantly changing.

The tavern's website boasts that the Trion lineup includes "familiar favorites and incredible imports to regional rarities and brand new brews."

Mayor Terry McDonald lauded Jacquay's Brew Haven efforts, which close down Broadway Street for one Saturday a year, as "a great way to draw 2,000 or so people to New Haven, to show that not all the fun stuff is in Fort Wayne." (Jacquay also led the city's $3.4 million downtown beautification

A New Haven haven for fans of craft beers, the Trion Tavern lays claim to the distinction as one of Allen County's oldest bars. *Courtesy* News-Sentinel.

project.) By 2016, Brew Haven was being billed as "northeast Indiana's premiere craft beer festival."

The Trion stakes a claim among Allen County's oldest bars; its name derives from the triumvirate of original owners as a tribute to their partnership. (The website also helpfully notes that the correct local pronunciation is "tree-on," not "try-on.") The tavern features seating for banquets and special events, accommodations for dart leagues and in-season sidewalk dining.

TROLLEY BAR

501–503 SOUTH CALHOUN STREET
2898 EAST DUPONT ROAD

The name "Trolley Bar" can evoke different sets of memories, depending on the age of the person doing the remembering. Some may even remember a time before the Trolly Bar added its *e*.

The Trolley Bar's ancestor, the Palm Gardens, opened downtown in 1890, states the website for the current restaurant, quoting an old postcard. "Superior and Calhoun Streets became the hub of entertainment circles," as well as a hub for the rapidly expanding network of electric trolleys, the

Shopoff's, at 12012 U.S. 24 West, is a family-run steakhouse. It has been in what it calls "the people pleasing business" since 1985. *Authors' collection.*

The neon sign of the Trolley Bar was a beacon to diners along Calhoun Street for decades. The fact that it was air-conditioned was a bonus. *Courtesy History Center.*

history adds. "Here was the beginning of the seven-mile Trolley ride to Robinson Park that opened in 1896. Here was the meeting place for those attending the Old League Ball Park north of the Armory. 'Meet me at the Trolley Bar Steak House' became more than a phrase; it became the name of the most popular restaurant in town." A newspaper piece refers to the Trolley Bar as downtown Fort Wayne's "dark, distinctive landmark."

From the mid-1950s to the mid-1970s, the piano bar and restaurant run by Robert Hadley was a favored hangout of the city's newspaper journalists and their visiting counterparts. "It wasn't unusual to see sportswriters from out of town munching and drinking there, particularly in the days before the Fort Wayne Zollner Pistons moved to Detroit," reported the *News-Sentinel's* Pat Parsley column. "The teams came, too. And, during the boys high school basketball tournament, out-of-town writers always said it was great to come to Fort Wayne because they could go to the Trolley Bar." Chef Lester Cartwright's legendary coleslaw was a tasty complement to many Trolley Bar meals.

Hadley died in 1997. About the same time, restaurateur Neal Summers was seeking a name for his new Dupont Road endeavor (he was already owner of the seafood restaurant Paula's on Main). He sought and got permission to revive the Trolley Bar name.

"You get lots of stories and memories when you bring up the Trolley Bar," Summers told a newspaper interviewer in 2000. "You hear about the jolliness of the place, the great times, all the smoke rolling around there."

In the days before Fort Wayne's railroad tracks were elevated at the direction of Mayor Harry Baals, the Trolley Bar sat next to a depot for the Nickel Plate Railroad. Behind the building is an old gas-holding structure. *Courtesy Creager Smith, Fort Wayne City Planning Department.*

This postcard dates to the early years of Bob Hadley's proprietorship of the Trolley Bar. Hadley ran the tavern between the mid-1950s and the mid-1970s. *Courtesy Randy Harter.*

Today's Trolley Bar—its full name Trolley Steaks and Seafood—is situated in a strip mall that deceptively masks a sleek, modern interior. The counter area originally featured seating on stools refurbished from the downtown Hobby House. And in another nod to the namesake, the servers' area was constructed to resemble a trolley ticket office.

The restaurant nearly succumbed to financial difficulties within months of its opening, until a rescuer stepped in. "Club Soda CEO Don Young… negotiated with the Dupont Place landlord and other key people (one) morning, and was able to keep the restaurant open. The Trolley Bar's 30 employees were retained. Most diners, apparently, were none the wiser," the *News-Sentinel* reported on September 25, 2001. These days, the Trolley Bar is in the hands of Rob and Stacy Clevenger. (The couple also acquired the southwest-side Chop's restaurant in 2016.)

2
Fun Food
(Burgers, Ice Cream and More)

ATZ'S ICE CREAM SHOPPE

211 EAST TILLMAN ROAD

Atz's Ice Cream Shoppe (including a second location on North Anthony Boulevard) closed in September 2014, ending more than fifty years of catering to Fort Wayne's sweet tooth. That followed the 2011 closure of Atz's ice-cream plant in Kendallville, a victim of aging and too-expensive-to-repair refrigeration equipment.

"Atz's was family," longtime customer Joan Hartwig told a WANE-TV interviewer. "We knew the waitresses by first name, they knew me. They were just dedicated people. If they saw my car, my coffee and water was on the table and the cook was fixing my breakfast. A lot of times, he would bring it out himself."

The family atmosphere was a product of family ownership. Atz's forerunner, Puritan Ice Cream, was founded by a trio of Fort Wayne men in 1922. Puritan's first home was in a former brewery abandoned to Prohibition; it was powered by a steam-driven engine. Ice was obtained throughout the winter from nearby Bixler Lake. By 1924, the company had built its own plant and attracted the interest of Frank Atz. He and his father-in-law would acquire the company in 1936. In addition to the two family shops, Atz supplied ice cream to groceries, supermarkets, drugstores, hospitals and schools within an hour's drive of Kendallville.

Atz's served both diner food and ice cream treats at two locations, one on North Anthony Boulevard and this one on Tillman Road. *Courtesy* News-Sentinel.

The Fort Wayne Atz stores were sandwich shops as well as ice-cream parlors. "Nothing very fancy, mind you," reminisced food reviewer Carol Tannehill, harking back to her childhood following a 2005 visit. "Just your basic bacon-and-egg breakfasts, daily specials, burgers, tuna melts and chicken salad plates."

The charm of the place, she said, was in its continuity. "The old coin-operated player piano is still there. So are the bay window, the patterned carpet, the farmhouse wallpaper, the lunch counter, the primitive antiques. Everything—the kitchen, the soda fountain, the serve-yourself freezer— is right where I remember it," she reminisced. And the same was true of the desserts. The "jewel-colored phosphates, make-your-own sundaes, eye-popping banana splits, big black cows, super-thick shakes, and sweetheart sodas garnished with whipped-cream towers, maraschino cherries and delicate pizelles" were just as she remembered.

AZAR'S

VARIOUS LOCATIONS

The only Big Boy restaurant in Fort Wayne today is located at 6800 Bluffton Road in Waynedale. But Big Boy has been a presence in the city since

1954. Brothers Alexander and David Azar began in the grocery business on Calhoun Street. (The family also owned a New Haven ice-cream stand.) They invested $1,000 and opened a store at 2440 West Jefferson Boulevard.

Within three decades, the business was worth more than $40 million and included twenty-six franchises in Indiana and Colorado. The Azar empire also included the railroad-themed Back 40 Junction restaurant in nearby Decatur and a pair of Marriott hotels, as well as several Taco Cabana restaurants and the Fort Wayne Marriott's Red River Steaks and BBQ.

Alex Azar credited the company's 1967 expansion into Denver with allowing it to see trends that were coming Fort Wayne's way. "Markets like Los Angeles and Denver usually help set the pattern for the nation," he told a newspaper interviewer in 1984. "So things customers out there have requested, like larger hamburgers, more salads or no-smoking areas, have been introduced here, too."

By the mid-1980s, the Azar's chain was so large that a commissary facility on Coliseum Boulevard prepared and distributed food to its area locations. Its bakery held the concession for St. Joseph's and Parkview Hospitals. The commissary was estimated to churn out 92,000 gallons of soup annually

Alex Azar's Big Boy restaurants once rivaled Hall's for dominance on the Fort Wayne food scene. The city's last remaining Big Boy restaurant is in Waynedale. *Courtesy* News-Sentinel.

and 400 gallons of pancake mix weekly. Azar's delivery trucks covered an estimated 109,000 miles in a year. The company workforce was listed at 2,100 and sales at $34.2 million.

By 2007, the Azar's empire had shrunk to the point that the commissary was no longer necessary. The building (with its plentiful warehouse and freezer storage space plus offices), as well as $200,000 in cash to cover upgrades, was donated to Community Harvest Food Bank. As food bank executive director Jane Avery told the story to the *News-Sentinel*: "When contacted last summer…regarding a donation from the Azar Co., she assumed, 'Good, more food.' She soon realized otherwise."

The company, now run by Alex's son George, focuses primarily on real estate investing and management. It continues to hold, though, the Waynedale Azar's, where the statue of the brawny lad hoisting a double-decker burger still greets you outside the front door, and the Back 40 Junction.

CINDY'S DINER

230 WEST BERRY STREET

Though it has moved several times through the decades, dedicated diners always know where to find Cindy's. And they know they might have to wait. After all, Cindy's slogan is "We serve the whole world, 15 at a time"—that is how many red-upholstered stools line the chrome diner's counter.

Cindy's currently sits a couple of blocks northwest of its longtime location at 830 South Harrison Street. The landmark was moved in June 2014 to make room for a large commercial/residential/parking complex, anchored by the headquarters of Ash Brokerage. While on Harrison Street, the diner was run by John Scheele and his wife—and the restaurant's namesake—Cindy.

"My husband bought it for me as a Mother's Day gift," she says.

The building, a 1952 Valentine model, was known by various names throughout the years: Noah's Ark (opened in 1954 at 1030 South Clinton Street), Paul's Diner, Jack's Diner and Marge's Diner following a move to 444 East Berry Street. Valentine, based in Wichita, Kansas, built small diners designed to be located along major highways. Neither of the Scheeles had any restaurant experience when the former seamstress and her building contractor spouse opened their rescued building in the fall of 1990.

Though relocated in 2014, Cindy's Diner still boasts of its onetime presence along the Lincoln Highway. If you look closely, you can see it boasts of Murphy's donuts as well. *Authors' collection.*

A treat of particular popularity at Cindy's is the doughnuts. They are made in a machine originally located at Fort Wayne's G.C. Murphy's store. The Scheeles quickly put in a claim when the Depot Café, which at the time was home to the machine, closed. Soon after they acquired their treasure, a man walked into Cindy's and told the Scheeles how he had put the machines together for Murphy's and had all the old recipes at home. He passed them along.

Cindy kept a guestbook—actually it grew to a pair of them—during her time running the diner. Among the names on the pages are those of bandleader Doc Severinsen, singer Marie Osmond and members of the Beach Boys, who did their Embassy Theatre concert wearing Cindy's Diner T-shirts the evening after their visit.

The Scheeles retired in May 2016. Ownership of Cindy's was assumed by Angie Harter, who began as a dishwasher in 1996 and worked her way up to general manager. "When it started, it was a job," Harter told a newspaper interviewer. "As I continued to work here and talk to all of the regulars, it became a home."

CONEY ISLAND

131 West Main Street

"Our buns are steamed," proclaims a sign at Coney Island, and that has been true since before World War I—1913 to be exact. On September 20 of that year, Harry Dorikis, James Samaras and Stilos Papas began grilling hot dogs in their newly opened diner. Not a lot has changed in the century-plus since, based on the premise of not messing with a good thing. Coney Island does not serve beer the way it did for a time post-Prohibition, but the same chili recipe has been used throughout the restaurant's existence.

Both morning and evening, the Main Street front window of Coney Island is a flurry of activity as workers assemble chili dogs for hungry customers. *Courtesy* News-Sentinel.

After the first two years, the original owners sold Coney Island to a group that included Vasil Eschoff; the restaurant has been in the hands of the Macedonian Eschoff and Choka families ever since. At the time of Coney Island's 2014 centennial, third-generation manager Kathy Choka recalled for a newspaper interviewer that "she talked her dad (then-owner Russ Choka) into letting her work there. She says it's so much more fun than working in an office, but she acknowledges at the end of the day she 'doesn't smell as good.' " (Coney Island employees chop seventy-five pounds of onions a day.) Kathy Choka's co-owner, Jimmy Todoran, is responsible for Coney Island's day-to-day operations.

It is estimated that daily sales are about 1,500 coneys; that number surges during the Christmas season as families come for a snack before or after viewing the beloved lighted Santa display on the nearby PNC Bank building. And it is believed that the farthest order was shipped to Orlando, Florida, to satisfy the craving of a contest winner for the meal of his choice; his pick was two dozen Coney Island hot dogs.

During the Blizzard of 1978, Coney Island played a role in helping the city dig out. On the restaurant's website, Rajib Jainagerker, the manager on Tuesday, Thursday and Saturday nights, recalls how a radio station announced that Coney Island was the only business open downtown. The restaurant was inundated with hungry snow-removal workers with Jainagerker (who retired in 2017) and one other server hustling to fill their orders.

As for famous customers, Mickey Mantle would rank right up there. The retired Yankees centerfielder stopped by one day in the late 1970s while visiting a friend in the area. The nearly $20 tip he is rumored to have left was evidence of his satisfaction with his meal.

The restaurant gained further distinction in May 2018 when *People* magazine's feature on the best coney dog in each of the fifty states chose Coney Island's dog as Indiana's representative. The magazine noted that Coney Island "still opens at 8 a.m., a time once set to accommodate overnight shift workers on their way home."

DAWSON'S

3915 SOUTH ANTHONY BOULEVARD

The opening of Dawson's was a sure sign of summer on the south side of Fort Wayne. Little changed over the years at the small octagonal stand with its pointed roof and red, white and yellow color scheme. That was thanks in part to the city's Board of Zoning Appeals, which repeatedly denied Dawson's requests to rebuild.

As many as 20 carhops would work delivering up to 1,500 hot dogs a day to hungry patrons. Many of those dogs were washed down with root beer served out of a wooden barrel.

Virginia Dawson ruled over her namesake root beer stand for twenty-three years before her 1976 retirement (the stand had originally opened in 1940). She was quoted in her 1991 obituary as having said: "I am not too old to work,

Curbside service—and frosty mugs of root beer—were always available during 1960s and 1970s summers at Dawson's south-side stand. *Courtesy* News-Sentinel.

but I'm getting a little old to work this hard. I wanted to stay open 25 years, but this year I saw so many people taking it easy and I realized that I haven't had a summer off in 23 years." For two and a half of those years, she also oversaw a pizza shop next door but gave it up when she found herself—like a pizza crust tossed once too often—stretched too thin.

The Dawson's lot was a place to gauge the coming of the Christmas season as well. For twenty years, Virginia sold trees to a loyal clientele.

After Dawson's retirement, the restaurant bearing her name reopened under new ownership and continued in operation into the 1990s. But even after the South Anthony landmark finally closed, its secret-recipe coney sauce could still be enjoyed for a time—first through a food truck and later at a since closed Dawson's Famous Coney Dogs restaurant.

The building that housed Dawson's was razed in April 2018 to make way for a Dollar General store.

GARDNER'S DRIVE-IN SANDWICH STAND

302 WEST JEFFERSON BOULEVARD

The idea for Gardner's took root in Springfield, Illinois. It was there in late 1934 or early 1935 that Francis W. Gardner, who had just graduated from college, took a job at his aunt's Icy Root Beer stand. He brought the concept back to Fort Wayne, where he opened a small, walk-up A&W location while he waited for his vision to rise nearby.

Gardner's, a white building with orange and black trim, opened in the fall of 1935. Inside seating was available at one of two U-shaped counters, each tended by its own waitress. But Gardner's was known for its "curb girls," who brought food and drinks on trays to drive-up customers. Mostly, people came for Gardner's uniquely cooked burgers. As Gardner's authority, Nola G. Marquardt described the preparation: "The meat was first fried at a very hot temperature, creating a glossy crust on one side. Then it was turned over and finished at a lower temperature so that the underside of the burger gave the appearance of being steamed."

In that more formal era, everything but the paper-wrapped hamburgers was served on chinaware and in glasses. That made the dishes popular souvenirs among drive-up diners and quickly led to the discontinuation of the free mini-mugs of root beer for young children. Curb girls got so frustrated by the thefts that they began taking down customers'

An early-1950s makeover made Gardner's an even more popular drive-in destination for downtown diners. The Lincoln Tower is among the landmarks looming in the background. *Courtesy Randy Harter.*

The circa 1940s Gardner's menu board featured a photograph of its steak hamburger sandwich with its toasted bun open to show the burger with a slice of onion and a pair of pickles. *Courtesy Randy Harter.*

license plate numbers. Offenders received a polite nudge from Gardner's attorney Walter E. Helmke (father of future Fort Wayne mayor Paul Helmke). His letter gently prodded offenders to return the items Helmke was certain the customer had "inadvertently" taken. "We are positive that this is purely an oversight on your part and would appreciate it very much if you would be so kind as to return the tray and glasses as soon as possible," the letter concluded.

Another popular menu item was a frozen chocolate malt that became known as a "frosty." It is easy to imagine future Wendy's founder Dave Thomas, an employee of the nearby Hobby House, fondly recalling this Gardner's treat as he crafted the menu for his new restaurant. Gardner's "Mr. Big" sandwich, a double-decker hamburger with a third slice of bun to separate the patties (its special sauce was tartar), foreshadowed another eventual fast-food staple.

Fort Wayne historian Betty Stein recalls a special memory of Gardner's that had more do with the place than the food:

> *Shortly after the war ended…I took my very young son there for a treat. As we sat in the car with the windows open (this was long before air-conditioning in homes or in cars), a young man in uniform and on crutches walked slowly toward the restaurant. "Hey, Mom, look. That man has only one leg," my son said excitedly. I tried to shush him, but the young man turned and said, "Don't stop him. It's the first time anyone has been honest. People pretend all the time. It's a relief to have someone tell the truth." I learned a lesson that day.*

In 1954, Gardner's management decided that expansion was warranted. So, a new steel-frame structure went up around the original wood-frame building. After June 12 of that year, drivers on Jefferson Boulevard would be met by a sign spelling "Gardner's Hamburgers" that dominated the front façade. Gardner's also expanded its reach to include a north restaurant at Coliseum Boulevard and California Road and a south restaurant on Covington Road. Neither reached the level of success of the original downtown location.

It was a signal that the good times were rapidly coming to a close. As Marquardt (daughter and granddaughter of the business's owners) tells it: "In the mid-1950s the drive-in era was in decline. Television had created an adult stay-at-home population.…Teenagers took over the curb business but they clogged the lot, had a great time but spent little. Oddly enough most of the nostalgia created about drive-ins has sprung from the very people responsible for their demise."

And Frank Gardner once told an interviewer: "We had to hire one of the meanest cops in town to keep law and order in our parking lot. The atmosphere had changed, and so the adults didn't patronize us like they used to…and TV was about to take over, so people could stay home in the evening."

By the mid-1960s, Gardner Enterprises had dissolved into bankruptcy. The Gardner family remained in the restaurant business, founding the Char-King chain, noted for its Charkey hamburger steak and Henny Penny fried chicken, in 1957. That chain was sold to Azar's in 1971.

But the Gardner's hamburger would live on, thanks to Gerhard and Evelyn Heinecke. The menu at their Harlan House Café and, later, Lunch Box Café advertised "all hamburgers—Gardner's style." And Gerhard would know; he began working at the downtown restaurant in 1955, three years after arriving from Northeim, Germany, with his parents and younger brother.

"I was 16 years old and couldn't speak hardly any English," he recalled in 1997. His job consisted of toasting buns, helping with the fries and, of course, frying those burgers.

True to tradition, Gerhard remained cagey about just what makes a hamburger a Gardner's hamburger. "It's the way it's prepared on the grill," he told an interviewer. "Pressed. Seared on the grill and removed with a sharp spatula. And—a few extra ingredients are secret."

LIBERTY DINER

2929 Goshen Road

Since 2000, George Smyrniotis has been offering Fort Wayne diners a bite of the Big Apple. His Liberty Diner, richly appointed with Statues of Liberty and other New York City reminders, is in a conveniently situated corner building just off Interstate 69 that formerly housed an Azar's Big Boy.

In fact, it was George Azar who was responsible for luring the native of Greece to Fort Wayne, following stints Smyrniotis spent running diners in New York City and Chicago. Smyrniotis attributes his success to Liberty Diner's "good food and good people working here…many from Day 1." The "family first" philosophy has resulted in loyalty from chefs, line cooks and the wait staff. The dedication starts at the top. "I can do anything in the restaurant," Smyrniotis says. It was he who passed on the preparation of his

The New York vibe is apparent in the sign for Liberty Diner. Could this lady with a lamp be holding a glass instead? *Authors' collection.*

grandmother Sophia's lemon rice soup and so many other recipes. "I'm on top of it, food-wise," says the self-professed workaholic.

Other details, such as soda straw caddies, add to Liberty's diner vibe. And on Fridays, patrons can partake of another facet of the diner experience like in the City that Never Sleeps—24-hour service.

Liberty Diner's massive menu is stuffed with what Hoosier restaurant authority Reid Duffy refers to as "Mom-tested nostalgia dishes," such as meatloaf, turkey and dressing and fried chicken. Smyrniotis's eclectic touch has also resulted in offerings from Italian (lasagna and ravioli) to seafood (crab cakes and mahi mahi).

LINCOLN TOWER SODA FOUNTAIN

116 EAST BERRY STREET

The Lincoln Tower is the Art Deco centerpiece of Downtown Fort Wayne. After its 1930 completion, the twenty-two-story Lincoln Tower enjoyed several decades as the tallest building in the state of Indiana (to the tip of its flagpole, the tower rises 312 feet from street level). The lunch counter tucked in next to the north entrance on Berry Street is an easily overlooked gem.

These days, the counter is watched over by sisters Vicki Statler and Teresa Pflueger, with an assist from their brother, Danny Roach. The business was acquired by the siblings' mother, Ilene Roach Stine, who manned the counter for twenty-seven years after her 1985 purchase.

Lincoln Tower memorabilia is prominent in the soda fountain's close quarters, as is a marble fireplace that graces the west wall. Many of the entrees prepared by the sisters in a deft display of choreography are named

The Lincoln Tower Soda Fountain is a popular lunch spot for those who toil at the Allen County Courthouse. The courthouse's proximity is apparent in this photograph, which also offers a sense of the memorabilia on display inside. *Authors' collection.*

after frequent patrons; many of those patrons come from the neighboring Allen County Courthouse. The menu features soups, salads, cold sandwiches such as egg salad and other sandwiches heated in a panini press. Baked goods are also available, as is caramel corn from the Wayne Street Gourmet Popcorn Shoppe. A phosphate or a cherry Coke might draw others to the soda fountain.

THE MUNCHIE EMPORIUM
(MAD ANTHONY BREWING COMPANY)

1109 TAYLOR STREET AND 2002 BROADWAY

If any two words summon up the Munchie experience, they might well be *Scooby snacks*. They are really just glorified steak fries—sprinkled with Old Bay seasoning and served with a cucumber-based dipping sauce—but they are enough to make you exclaim "Jinkies!" or even "Zoinks!"

These days, the Munchie is known as the Mad Anthony Brewing Company. The brewpub trend arrived in Fort Wayne in 1998 as Mark Melchi's Munchie opened its doors to Blaine Stuckey and his Mad Anthony brand. A deli area was converted to a fermentation area capable of brewing 280 gallons of beer in a batch. Production at the multi-tank, four-fermenter facility was overseen by brewmaster Todd Grantham; today, output has increased to more than 2,500 barrels of beer annually.

The dining room lays claim to another piece of Fort Wayne history; it was the location of the city's first Kroger grocery store.

The decorations are best described as 1960s kitsch. "From the classic Drewry's Mountie that welcomes you to the Nixon booth to the signs, knick knacks and 60's memorabilia, visitors are immersed in a time long (since) passed," is how the Mad Anthony website describes it. "Mid-Century Mayhem" was reviewer Carol Tannehill's phrase. "This mess…welcomes you warmly at the door like an old college chum," she added. "It invites you to come as you are, flop down at a second-hand table covered with oilcloth and drink a beer or two."

Also part of the décor is the ceiling memorializing members of the Heineken Club, those who have drunk at least a dozen of the Dutch ale. Look for the asterisks; they denote those who polished off their dozen in a single sitting (not counting bathroom breaks).

The Mad Anthony Brewing Company and the Munchie Emporium joined forces in 1998 to open Fort Wayne's first brewpub. *Courtesy* News-Sentinel.

Over the years, Mad Anthony has evolved into a regional concern, with locations in Warsaw, Angola and Auburn as well as Fort Wayne. Offerings include Olde Fort Blonde Lager, Ol' Woody Pale Ale and seasonal brews such as Summer Daze and Snowplowed Winter Ale.

POWERS HAMBURGERS

1402 SOUTH HARRISON STREET

Other cities have their White Castle hamburgers; Fort Wayne has its Powers Hamburgers.

The city was one of several in the regional burger empire of brothers Leo, Clell, Harold and Dale Powers, who started in Dearborn, Michigan, in 1935. They opened locations in Port Huron, Grand Rapids, Detroit and—in 1940—Fort Wayne. Leo was the proprietor, along with his wife, Esther. The Fort Wayne location was strategically situated within sight of one of the city's largest employers, Lincoln National Life Insurance. The city's main post office was also a neighbor.

A somewhat spartan dining area comprises eighteen stools and a lone booth. In 2006, restaurant reviewer Carol Tannehill captured Powers thusly: "In an ever-changing world, it's wonderful to stop at Powers and have hamburgers that taste just as they used to when I was 6 and 12 and 24. I remember going there with my daddy, with my high school classmates, with my first boyfriend."

Hungry patrons continue to queue up for the square mini burgers slathered with onions. Those who are regulars might have a coffee cup stashed under the counter, awaiting their next visit. But the days of 24-hour operation are in the past. And a second Fort Wayne Powers Hamburgers, started by Leo and Esther on Maumee Avenue in 1947, closed in 2004. A third operated in the city in the 1980s.

The Powerses' son Rolin took over running the business in 1980. He died a decade later, and his sister Marilyn Penick stepped in. Michael Hall assumed ownership in 1999. Though the business is no longer in the family, the Powers name, and those signature three-bite burgers, remain the same, as does the black-and-white porcelain shell of a building, described by one profiler as "like some Edward Hopper nighthawks-at-the-diner painting."

Burger expert George Motz (author of *Hamburger America*) had high praise for Powers in an interview with the *Indianapolis Star*. He called Powers "one of the greatest slider emporiums in America, one of the finest examples of the original American hamburger."

"My burger contains DNA from the first burgers that were made at White Castle and White Tower, all those White restaurants back in the '20s, and Powers is still making that burger," Motz added. "A very important piece of American history right in Fort Wayne."

WHIPPY DIP

209 EAST SOUTH STREET, MONROEVILLE

"Come as you are & leave cool & refreshed." The Whippy Dip delivers on this promise whether you elect to eat at one of the nearby half-dozen picnic seats or drive through and take your treats with you. The drive-through, by the way, is speakerless. Make your selection, pull up to the window and they will fill your order while you wait.

Burgers and coneys, fries and onion rings and that Indiana favorite, the breaded tenderloin, have been staples since the Whippy Dip's opening

Smitty's Tasty Burger Shop was located at 128 West Jefferson Boulevard. Today, it is the site of a Hilton hotel, across Jefferson from the Foellinger-Freimann Botanical Conservatory. *Courtesy Randy Harter.*

Residents of Monroeville and surrounding areas—not to mention their four-legged friends—have cooled off on many a summer's day with the treats available at the Whippy Dip. *Courtesy* News-Sentinel.

(under a different name) in 1973. Even your dog is treated right. You can get him or her a small cup of vanilla ice cream, topped off with a Milk-Bone.

In 2014, Mary and Jeff Knoblauch celebrated twenty years of running the Whippy Dip, with Mary managing the staff of about fifteen, mostly students. Before buying the stand, Mary had been a factory worker; she longed for a job where her children could accompany her to work.

The Whippy Dip's ice cream is made on-site. Among the other homemade treats are the coney sauce, coleslaw, brownies, cookies and cookie dough that can be used to top various frozen treats.

The Whippy Dip is open from March through September.

ZESTO'S

2225 BROADWAY
5740 FALLS DRIVE
6218 ST. JOE CENTER ROAD
210 EAST WASHINGTON CENTER ROAD
10897 ISABELLE DRIVE, NEW HAVEN

For many Fort Wayne residents, the annual mid-March opening of Zesto's ice-cream stand signals an end to winter hibernation.

The anchor store at the intersection of Broadway and Creighton Street is a landmark to locals. They are welcomed by its distinctive blue-and-white striped paint scheme and the sign topped by a vanilla cone.

Since the opening of this first store at Broadway and Creighton Avenue, Zesto's has been a go-to destination for summer refreshment. Residents across northeast Indiana have been able to join in the enjoyment. *Authors' collection.*

The local, family-owned chain has expanded to include Zesto's in Huntington, Angola, Warsaw, Bluffton and New Haven, in addition to four locations throughout Fort Wayne. Local franchiser Sebastian Diettrich began the expansion with the opening of Fort Wayne's second Zesto's, at the northside Coldwater Crossing, in 1991.

Nationally, Zesto's can be found in Nebraska, South Dakota, Louisiana, Georgia, Missouri and South Carolina. Missouri is where the chain got its start in the post–World War II years, as the Taylor Freezer Company perfected its Zest-o-Mat frozen custard machine.

3

A Little More Upscale

CHAPPELL'S CORAL GRILLE

6328 West Jefferson Boulevard
2723 Broadway

The Coral Grille, opened in 1988, was an extension of Chappell's Seafood Market, which started in 1985. The Coral Grille's dining room was dominated by a twenty-one-foot-long mahogany bar, highlighted by intricate hand carvings and a giant mirror. The bar was built sometime between 1848 and 1860 and was rumored to have graced the screen in several John Wayne Westerns. Ghosted Coca-Cola and drugstore advertisements remain visible

Chappell's has moved from Broadway to its current Covington Plaza location; the seafood remains a signature draw. The restaurant debuted an extensive renovation in 2017. *Courtesy* News-Sentinel.

today on the building's north-facing brick façade. The circa 1890 building itself boasts a link to Hollywood history; at one time, it housed a grocery run by Ott Peters, an uncle of 1930s screen legend and Fort Wayne native Carole Lombard.

Chappell's now resides in southwest Fort Wayne's Covington Plaza, with the restaurant now billing itself as Chappell's Steaks and Seafood. A renovation completed in 2017 featured the addition of salad and hot bars, as well as installation of a free-standing fireplace.

Its website touts Chappell's as having "a bistro-style feel where people could relax and have a great experience." Market availability determines the menu choices, owner Gary Chappell says, so the selections change daily.

CLUB SODA

235 East Superior Street

Looking for a place to celebrate the ring-a-ding-ding hedonism of the Rat Pack era? You could do worse than a place that boasts: "There's nothing good for you here. Enjoy yourself. That's what we're about."

Those were the words of co-owner Jason Smith when Club Soda debuted in 1999. Smith and five fellow investors spent $1 million to transform the former Indiana Textile Company building. The faded advertisement for cheesecloth, beef cloth, cotton waste and "sanitized wiping cloths for every purpose" remains prominent on the building's eastern façade.

The building is adjacent to Headwaters Park and was acquired by Fort Wayne's Board of Public Works as part of the park's development phase. It

The former Indiana Textile Company building could have been a casualty of Headwaters Park development. But six investors bought it and turned Club Soda into one of Fort Wayne's hippest and hottest nightspots. *Authors' collection.*

was spared demolition because it did not fall within the floodplain. At the time, city redevelopment specialist Loren Kravig said, "We've been looking for the right kind of business to go into that building. (Club Soda) should be good for the park and, really, mutually beneficial." Two decades on, the investment has paid off for both sides.

The building's 6,300 square feet were made over under the supervision of architect Alan Grinsfelder (who has contributed to the design of several other Fort Wayne restaurants) and interior designer Patricia Baldus. The goal was the feel of a New York City loft—a loft that includes walnut bars on two floors, topped in limestone (Daniel Seyfert deserves the builder's credit). The top floor was outfitted with a gourmet kitchen.

The neon sign, a product of the Johnson Bros. in South Whitley, is designed to evoke an earlier era as well. Let Smith describe it: "It turns on with the pink neon Club Soda logo, then blue bubbles pop up."

The club's main level, which has seating for nearly eighty people, opens onto a deck that can seat nearly seventy more. Among the attractions on the inside is a restored Fort Wayne–made Packard piano. Club Soda's website summarizes the experience they want you to have—"sizzling steaks, cool jazz and commodious cocktails"—with the emphasis on martinis.

CORK 'N CLEAVER

221 East Washington Center Road

Cork 'N Cleaver has been one of Fort Wayne's special occasion restaurants since its opening in 1974. (The Cork 'N Cleaver chain began in 1964 in Scottsdale, Arizona. Cleaver-style menus highlight the steak, chop and seafood entree options.)

A particular highlight is the well-tended and well-stocked salad bar; among the higher-end offerings is caviar. The selections are eaten off chilled pewter plates. A 2003 newspaper review offered a comprehensive overview of the salad bar offerings:

> *Bowls teeming with head lettuce, tender spinach leaves and a blend of designer greens....All sorts of adornments—pepperoni slices, button mushrooms, gargantuan strawberries, chopped egg, shredded cheese, diced beets, bean sprouts, pepperoncini, cherry tomatoes, bacon pieces, black*

Cork 'N Cleaver is noted for, among other things, its caviar-stocked salad bar. The Fort Wayne location of the nationwide chain remains a destination for those seeking a more formal dining experience. *Authors' collection.*

olives, sunflower seeds, croutons and the usual dressings…potato salad, pasta salad, fruit salad [and] *creamed herring.*

The legacy of Cork 'N Cleaver is evident in one of the most upscale of Fort Wayne's restaurants, Eddie Merlot's. William Humphries's early restaurant experience was gained as a busboy at Cork 'N Cleaver. After college, Humphries became a franchisee in Subway restaurants, opening his first in Fort Wayne in 1983. Today, he oversees 750 locations in Indiana and Ohio. His vision of Eddie Merlot's, which bills itself as "one of America's great steak houses," was realized in 2001; there are now restaurants in Indianapolis, Cincinnati, Chicago, Detroit, Pittsburgh, Denver and other locales.

DEBRAND FINE CHOCOLATES

10105 AUBURN PARK DRIVE
5608 COLDWATER ROAD
878 HARRISON STREET
4110 WEST JEFFERSON BOULEVARD (JEFFERSON POINTE)

From an early age, Cathy Brand-Beere had an interest in chocolate. Her parents ran the Country Kitchen, a cake and candy supplies store. In her teen years, she was assisting in candy-making classes and baking wedding cakes. But chocolate always drew her back; so much so that she made it her life's work. Her commitment to quality has landed her product in as faraway places as Europe and the Middle East, as well as into the hands of a future U.S. president.

DeBrand Fine Chocolates opened its first store in October 1987—in Brand's century-old childhood home. The business has grown to encompass four Fort Wayne locations and a worldwide shipping capability from its 30,000-square-foot, $2.5 million headquarters, which opened in 2003. The consistent color scheme is, as you might guess, a rich chocolate brown.

Brand-Beere's husband, Tim, had a hand in the planning and design of the headquarters. He is an architecture buff with a background in commercial art. Tim was so hands-on that he even spent time painting the store ceiling like Michelangelo in the Sistine Chapel—flat on his back on a scaffolding. The building also features three kitchens: one for cooking chocolate centers ("fresh crèmes, rich caramels, decadent ganaches, truffles, brittles, smooth creams and much more," according to the DeBrand website), a second devoted to making ice cream and DeBrand's Connoisseur collection chocolates, and the third for chocolate preparation and dipping.

Rigorous employee training is the key to ensuring a consistently enjoyable customer experience. And, as a bonus, employees get to eat their

Cathy Brand-Beere stands before the counter at one of her stylized DeBrand locations, where chocolate-colored walls are the décor of choice. *Courtesy* News-Sentinel.

faux pas. Brand-Beere believes packaging is as important as the product; some boxes are actually made of chocolate themselves. The goal for the chocolate remains as it always has: quality you can enjoy or give to someone else without busting your budget.

"Most people may not be able to afford the absolute best cars, vacations, diamonds…but most people can afford to treat themselves to the absolute best chocolate in an environment that makes them feel special," Brand-Beere once told a newspaper interviewer. And that philosophy was key to helping the company weather the Great Recession, she believes. "We stayed strong," she said in 2013. "I think it's a luxury item that's affordable."

Other items of note on the DeBrand's menu include coffee, hot chocolate, ice-cream sundaes and, in the fall, giant caramel apples. A section of the company's website is devoted to photographs of celebrities enjoying DeBrand's chocolates, from Jane Pauley to Demi Lovato to George Lopez. Among the other notable names are the princess of Dubai and Donald Trump. "DeBrand was hired to supply chocolates for 'The Apprentice' TV show, and now sells its product in most Trump properties," a 2012 profile of Brand-Beere in *Business People* magazine reported.

Everyday customers remain equally smitten. "By the appearance of the locations—you know it's cared for and top notch," customer Elena Soto was quoted as saying in 2010. "You are buying the brand, not just the chocolate….I just know I wouldn't go anywhere else in Fort Wayne to get my chocolate."

HARTLEY'S

4301 FAIRFIELD AVENUE

Like so many other great Fort Wayne restaurants, Hartley's was a family affair. Hartley McLeod Sr. and his wife, Wanda, were the original proprietors. They were assisted by son Hartley Jr. and daughter-in-law Sue. Daughter Pamela Downs, another part owner, trained the kitchen staff and eventually assumed ownership herself.

Hartley Sr. founded his namesake casual fine dining bistro in 1983. His name was already familiar to Fort Wayne residents as a hockey player with the Komets in the 1950s. After hanging up his skates, the Canada native elected to stay in the city and found work with the Yacht Club and

Though small in size, Hartley's was big on the list of family-run eateries that catered to the tastes of Fort Wayne diners. *Courtesy* News-Sentinel.

the Hoosier Tavern. McLeod converted a former ice-cream parlor to fit his vision. Indiana restaurant authority Reid Duffy noted that Hartley's menu included "a Hoosier rarity—sauteed frog legs."

Hartley's closed in 2009, after Downs had contemplated relocating from the largely residential neighborhood the restaurant had called home. The *News-Sentinel* reported that Downs "was reluctant to relocate because the family has so many memories connected to the Fairfield building."

Hartley Jr. and Sue McLeod went on to start a restaurant at the Bridgewater Golf Club in nearby Auburn.

OYSTER BAR

1830 SOUTH CALHOUN STREET

The Oyster Bar did not become an oyster bar until the mid-1950s, when then owner Hughie Johnston, also first baseman on the Zollner Piston softball team, introduced the delicacy.

Reid Duffy's Guide to Indiana's Favorite Restaurants offers this earlier history:

> *The Oyster Bar's narrow two-story building traces its dining roots to 1888 as a neighborhood watering hole founded by one Ferdinand Oetting. From 1894 to 1944, it was (a) family affair under the auspices of Joseph Schnee, who tenaciously guided the operation through the twin whammies of Prohibition and the Depression, with the help of his famously cantankerous son, Leo.*

Steve Gard has built the Oyster Bar into one of Fort Wayne's finest, a restaurant that packs a lot of charm and class into a small space. *Courtesy* News-Sentinel.

Historian David Lupke reports that Schnee and his wife, Rosina, lived above the Oyster Bar for sixteen years while running the restaurant.

The *News-Sentinel* recounted another unusual Oyster Bar tale: the night in 1976 when a would-be robber was killed there. A bar patron was seriously wounded by a ricocheting bullet; the injured man was a prosecutor who had gained a conviction of the shooter in a previous robbery. For many years, a bullet hole in the Oyster Bar's back door served as a reminder of that night.

In the mid-1980s, the Oyster Bar was acquired by present owners Steve and Brenda Gard. As Steve Gard told a newspaper interviewer, personal service has been his hallmark. "If there's a problem with the way the food was prepared, there's no charge," he said. "If there was something wrong with the service, I would either comp the meal, buy a round of drinks or buy (them) a dessert."

Close quarters are part of the Oyster Bar's charm. The front room seats thirty-eight, with another ten at the bar. The back room, accessible only by shimmying past the chefs in the galley kitchen, seats eighteen.

PAULA'S ON MAIN

1732 WEST MAIN STREET

Paula's has survived ownership upheaval and a series of legal entanglements to emerge as an upscale Nebraska neighborhood seafood staple.

The business started as Lindi's Gourmet Market and Deli in April 1991, a partnership that included, among others, former Chappell's general manager Lindi Miller and Paula Brown. By September 1993, a falling out led to Miller's departure and the renamed Paula's Seafood.

Neal Summers, another member of the ownership group, drew the wrath of neighborhood residents when he sought an alcohol permit for Lindi's in 1992. They feared Summers's envisioned Mangy Moose Saloon, part of a 3,200-square-foot expansion of the restaurant, would add to the raucousness of the five bars already along Main Street.

The alcohol permit and the expansion went through, but a plan to incorporate the train cars of the closed Depot Café never materialized. By July 2001, Summers had departed the ownership group for his revival of the Trolley Bar. Brown, by now Paula Brown Phillips, departed as her namesake restaurant was taken over by Don Young.

Young abruptly closed Paula's on August 18, 2003. Phillips reacquired the business in partnership with Frank Casagrande and Tom Sokolik, owners of the nearby O'Sullivans Italian Pub. The rechristened Paula's on Main has been back in business since late 2004. The building houses both the restaurant and a market, where "if the fish were any fresher they'd be swimming."

The Paula's on Main compound of restaurant and seafood market dominates the west end of Main Street. *Authors' collection.*

Miller has remained active on the Fort Wayne restaurant scene as well. Her Deli 620 was in business for about fifteen years, first on Calhoun Street and later in the PNC Bank building. That endeavor ended in December 2016. But the spring of 2018 saw the opening of Lindi's, returning Miller to Main Street but this time downtown.

"I didn't want to be done," Miller told an interviewer, "even when I closed. I love what I do."

The location offers limited seating—sixteen patrons at pink booths and white tables—but has quickly become a takeout destination spot with its soups, sandwiches and expansive salad bar.

THE RIB ROOM

1235 EAST STATE BOULEVARD

Its website touted the Rib Room as "a Fort Wayne tradition since 1957, reinvented 2016."

In 1957, Von Filippou and Nick Stamanis paid $20,000 for the Del-Mar Bar and converted it to Nick's Rib Bar. (Von, just five years removed from his native Greece, was not yet a U.S. citizen; his name was added a year later after he was naturalized.) The restaurant passed into the hands of Filippou's son Sam and Sam's brother-in-law; they ran it from 1992 until 2015, when the restaurant closed. When Sam Filippou died in July 2017, his obituary noted he had been a Green Beret in the U.S. Army, "one of his proudest achievements." The obituary also made note of his degree in microbiology from Indiana University and that "he was known for cooking 'the best filet in town.' "

In the 2006 edition of *Reid Duffy's Guide to Indiana's Favorite Restaurants*, the author says the Rib Room served "four thousand pounds of ribs a week, along with…two thousand pounds of French fries, eight hundred pounds of baked potatoes, and three hundred pounds of hash browns."

The Henry brothers—Chris, Matt and Kurt—purchased the building immediately west of the Rib Room in 2014, converting it into a wine and martini bar they christened Nick's. (The name is an homage to the original 1957 restaurant.) The next year, they took over the Rib Room business as well. A remodel brought the restaurant's look into the twenty-first century, and the Henrys wisely decided to keep the menu largely as it was when they reopened in March 2016. General manager Karon

Left: Refurbished and reopened in 2016, the Rib Room offers a nighttime noir-ish vibe to East State Boulevard. The sign for Fort Wayne's last remaining Pio's Market is partly visible as well. *Courtesy Daniel Baker.*

Below: Before the Rib Room was the Rib Room, the building was the first branch of the Fort Wayne National Bank (the 2016 renovation uncovered the bank's vault, among other treasures). The sign for one of Fort Wayne's Pio's Markets is partly visible as well. *Courtesy Bob Baker.*

Messman says all the restaurant's proprietary sauces and dressings remained unchanged.

Christina Filippou, granddaughter of Von, was a consultant on the renovations and served as dining room manager. The Rib Room is where she grew up, and it is where she remembers drinking virgin daiquiris with her grandfather behind the bar. (A vintage Rib Room menu notes: "Sorry, under Indiana Excise Law we are unable to serve minors.") The restaurant is also where the family celebrated all its holidays.

In a Facebook post announcing the reopening, the Henry brothers wrote:

> *We cannot thank Fort Wayne residents enough for the outpouring of support that they have shown toward the Rib Room by way of phone call, in-person visits, and social media inquiries. It was this encouragement from the regular clientele, neighborhood patrons, and special occasion diners that helped us come to the conclusion that this Fort Wayne tradition should not come to an end.*

Messman, who describes the remodeled Rib Room's style as "modern rustic," says the update uncovered some interesting details. The building that houses the Rib Room was originally the first branch office of Fort Wayne National Bank. As drywall was stripped away, Mossman said a distinctive I-beam was exposed, as was the former bank's vault. That area now serves as restrooms for the Rib Room.

In an interview with *Fort Wayne* magazine, Petros Gounaris, a onetime goat herder in Greece, claimed in mock exasperation to have no knowledge of the Rib Room's signature barbecue sauce recipe. "Nobody knows when Petros comes, nobody knows when Petros goes," Karon Messman told an interviewer. "We just know that his barbecue sauce magically appears."

The revival was to be short-lived. The Henrys' incarnation of the Rib Room closed at the end of 2017, but the opening of Sweet Lou's Pizza kept the building in the restaurant business as well as in the family. Lou Henry, nephew to Chris, Matt and Kurt, specialized in deep-dish pizzas, and those ribs remained on the menu. Unfortunately, Sweet Lou's closed at the end of 2018.

SUMMIT CLUB

110 WEST BERRY STREET

From 1971 to 2009, if you had friends in high places, they might have treated you to a meal at one of the highest places in Fort Wayne. The Summit Club offered what it advertised as "fine dining with a spectacular view." Located on the twenty-fifth and twenty-sixth floors of what is now the PNC Bank building, it delivered on both promises.

The richly appointed, sumptuously paneled club offered a full-city view and featured two main dining areas: the grill and the main dining room. Private rooms were available for business meetings or wedding receptions. Total seating was about 350 people.

Above: Huntington native Dan Quayle, vice president and Indiana senator, addresses a gathering at the Summit Club. Among those listening is three-term Fort Wayne mayor Paul Helmke (at Quayle's right elbow). *Courtesy* News-Sentinel.

Left: In addition to gleaming coffee urns, the Summit Club offered some of the finest views available of Fort Wayne, standing even taller than the twenty-two-story Lincoln Tower. *Courtesy* News-Sentinel.

The Summit Club was ultimately a casualty of the Great Recession, which led to a downturn in membership. It had billed itself on its website as an "exclusive, private members club for personal and professional business men and women."

The two floors of the Summit Club have seen a renaissance with the opening of Gary Probst and Julia Fiechter's Empyrean Events and Catering. Touches added during the renovation include a water wall.

4

Ethnic Restaurants

BANDIDO'S

8230 Glencairn Boulevard, Aboite
4122 Lima Road, Glenbrook
6536 East State Boulevard, Georgetown
7510 Winchester Road, Waynedale

Strategically located throughout the city, Bandido's has Fort Wayne's craving for Mexican food covered. (Those headed to Ohio can also get their fix at a Bandido's in Lima.)

In 2013, Jimmy Schindler II bought the business his father had started in the 1980s. (Hank Freistroffer was among the elder Schindler's co-investors.) The elder Schindler switched from his Jimmie's Pizza to Mexican after recognizing the start of a trend. He and his wife had gone out for dinner and noticed a line around the block at the Mexican place where they ate. So, he switched gears and opened his first Bandido's on Winchester Road.

The younger Schindler has chosen to emphasize a theme of "Fresh Made Daily." The restaurants' website lays out the philosophy:

> *We hand-chop our pico de gallo throughout the day. At Bandidos, you won't*
> *find any canned beans or processed cheese dip. We slow-cook our pinto*

Owner Jimmy Schindler II rededicated the Bandido's chain to a "Fresh Made Daily" philosophy after acquiring the restaurants from his father in 2013. *Authors' collection.*

beans from scratch every single day and we make our queso dips using real cheese from Midwest farms. It's all fresh, and it's all made daily. Come taste the difference at Bandidos.

BLACKIE'S CORRAL RIB BAR

2713 SOUTH CALHOUN STREET

The Ochoa brothers, Panfilo and Pantaleon, are credited with introducing Fort Wayne to Mexican cuisine in the late 1960s, according to Panfilo's ("Blackie") 2007 obituary. At the height of their food's popularity, the brothers also operated Blackie's restaurants on Decatur Road, Fairfield Avenue and in New Haven.

The Ochoa family came to Fort Wayne from Laredo, Mexico, in 1951 as migrant farm workers. Pantaleon, also known as Junior, had preceded the family north a year earlier and had settled into a job at International Harvester. "There was work here and promise, and the chance for a man to make something of a life for him and his children," Junior recalled.

In 1960, Blackie opened a bar at Wallace Street and Weisser Park Avenue. Eight years later, he made the move to Calhoun Street. Family members assisted him in making the business transition from bar to restaurant. By

1984, brother Joe, also part of the management team, lauded Fort Wayne's progress in diversity. "This is a much different place than it used to be," he said. "Anywhere I want to go, I can go, and everywhere I go I've got a friend there."

These days, La Margarita ("Famous for our blue margaritas," it says over the door) continues the Mexican food tradition at the Calhoun Street location.

CAFÉ JOHNELL

2529 SOUTH CALHOUN STREET

Though it has been closed since 2001, Café Johnell remains one of Fort Wayne's most renowned restaurants. For more than twenty-five years, Café Johnell was a fixture in the "Guide to Fine Dining" published by *Travel-Holiday* magazine; it also was a consistent four-star recommendation in the *Mobil Travel Guide*.

John Spillson (son of Berghoff Gardens owner Nicholas Spillson) served in the U.S. Merchant Marine during World War II and returned to his hometown to work at the then thriving General Electric plant. Following his entrepreneurial interest, he founded Johnelli's Pizza in 1958. Three years later, he decided to convert the pizzeria into a fine dining restaurant. John and his wife, Jayne, settled on red velvet upholstery and linen tablecloths. Those theatrical touches, as well as Café Johnell's rococo-framed artwork, were no doubt influenced by Jayne's acting background. The restaurant's entry door had been repurposed from the city's Rockhill Mansion.

Shortly after John Spillson's 1995 death, columnist Nancy Nall eulogized him by capturing the Café Johnell experience:

> *It was a place where you dressed for dinner and paid for the privilege, but it never disappointed. Café Johnell served real French food, heavy on the butter and sauces and the tongue-twisting entrees, but of a quality that could stand up with Chicago's best restaurants....If (John) Spillson couldn't say, 'Billions and billions served,' he could say, 'Thousands and thousands wowed.' Those people know more about food because he fed them. They expect more from a dining experience because he fed them.*

Left: John N. Spillson took care to make sure his French cuisine was paired with the finest of wines. On one special occasion in 1986, he acquired a $3,000 red Bordeaux bottled in 1874 at southern France's Chateau Latour. *Courtesy Randy Harter.*

Below: Nike, John N. and Jon Spillson were responsible for maintaining the consistent four-star quality of Café Johnell. As they described it, "Cuisine Excellente…Dans Une Atmosphere Elegante. (Excellent food…in an elegant atmosphere.)" *Courtesy Randy Harter.*

Marcus Spillson carried on his family's restauranting tradition when he opened his 07 Pub at the intersection of Broadway and Bluffton Road. *Authors' collection.*

Others were equally laudatory, noting that Spillson was a vocal advocate on a range of restaurant issues. "He was an innovator in this area of the country," said Jerry Wilson, a former Fort Wayne Country Club chef. "He was respected all over the United States. They even knew about him in France." Added the Summit Club's managing director Christian Frappier, "He stood up for what he believed in. I knew about his reputation for quality long before I even came to Fort Wayne."

The restaurant remained in the family. Daughter Nike Spillson, a French-trained chef, took over for the final six years. Her brother Jon continued to serve as Café Johnell's wine master. After the restaurant closed, the building was sold and converted into a Mexican restaurant. Residents of Fort Wayne's Woodview Healthcare facility became the grateful recipients of Nike Spillson's culinary skills.

And now a fourth generation has carried on the family tradition; Marcus Spillson's 07 Pub opened in 2017.

Marcus, who grew up washing dishes at Café Johnell, is keenly attuned to the history his name carries. Framed photographs and other mementoes of the Berghoff Gardens and Café Johnell grace the exposed-brick walls of his pub at 3516 Broadway. Portions of the bar consist of reclaimed wood from the building's former dance floor, while another section was part of the basketball court at South Side High School.

Marcus says he felt the pull of home after spending years chasing titles for oil and gas leases in places like Houston and Tulsa. He put that talent to use tracing the history of his own building, a bar he frequented as a youth. His sleuthing uncovered that Lot 38 in Broadway Park has nearly a one-hundred-year history as everything from a subdivided ice-cream parlor/barbershop to the Germania Grill; in the run-up to World War II, the name was changed to the Old Mill Grill and Bar.

The building was constructed under the supervision of A.M. Strauss, a renowned Fort Wayne architect also in charge of the Lincoln Tower and the Emboyd (now Embassy) Theatre. The Kendallville native is also credited with more than a dozen buildings on Indiana University's Bloomington campus. Marcus Spillson's 07 building, named for the ZIP code of the neighborhood where he grew up and that he again calls home, features the door to a reclaimed walk-in cooler and a tin ceiling that had been covered by acoustic tiles.

Marcus covered the reclaimed ceiling with copper-colored paint that features metallic flecks. You may not be able to see those flecks from floor level, Marcus says, but he knows they are there. It is the attention to detail you would expect from Fort Wayne restaurant royalty.

CASA D'ANGELO

CASA 6340 STELLHORN ROAD

The Casa Restaurant Group also includes
Casa, 7545 West Jefferson Boulevared
Casa Ristoranti Italiano, 4111 Parnell Avenue
Casa Grille, 401 East Dupont Road

Ask a Fort Wayne resident to name a local restaurant. If they do not name a Hall's restaurant, chances are their first choice will be a Casa D'Angelo's instead. The chain has been around since 1977, the year Tom Casaburo traded in his law enforcement career based largely on a newspaper advertisement.

Casaburo had been Fort Wayne's director of public safety and had also worked for the Federal Bureau of Investigation (FBI). He was set to take a job in New York as director of law enforcement for the state's parks system, but budget constraints put that position on hold.

Over coffee one morning, Casaburo and friend Jim D'Angelo started chatting about an advertisement for a vacant restaurant location near Glenbrook Square. As Casaburo told an interviewer in 2004: "As long as we'd known each other, we'd enjoyed cooking and, more importantly, eating Italian food." D'Angelo had friends who ran Cunetto's Restaurant in St. Louis, which used the Italian recipes of Grandma D'Angelo, so he and Casaburo set out on an apprenticeship. They came back every bit as enthused, and a dynasty took root.

The Casa Grille on Stellhorn Road is one of the more recent members of the Fort Wayne staple Italian restaurant chain. *Authors' collection.*

"I cooked, my wife, Sharon, washed the pots and made the lasagna, and Jim worked the front," Casaburo said.

In the early 1990s, right around the time D'Angelo retired, the Casaburos launched an ambitious expansion plan. Their second location, in southwest Fort Wayne, opened in 1993.

The Casa chain now numbers four restaurants, all featuring what reviewer Carol Tannehill called Casa's "basics—delicious pasta, filling portions, reasonable prices and the celebrated signature salad."

The Casaburos also operated the now closed TJ's Pasta on Coliseum Boulevard. And their former restaurant on Fairfield Avenue, which had once been home to Ted Gouloff's Paramount Grill, closed in 2010. It is now home to the trendy Wunderkammer art gallery.

In another review, Tannehill indulged in a little alternate history and tried to picture a world without Casa: "I envisioned all those business lunches, after-work carryouts, microwaved leftovers, charity benefits, dinner dates and catered parties that would be forever sad and salad-less. I shuddered at my post-apocalyptic vision."

HAINAN HOUSE

1820 BLUFFTON ROAD

Diem Huynh and her husband, Chien Tran, opened the Hainan House at Quimby Village in 1989. The intricately carved three-dimensional artwork

Hainan House adds to the eclectic culinary mix that exists in Quimby Village. The Bluffton Road strip also features Mexican, the original Hall's Drive-In, and a Burger King. *Authors' collection.*

on the walls and the exotically stocked aquarium in the center of the dining room add visual interest. (An October 2011 kitchen fire led to a three-month freshening up of the interior.) Among the dishes adding interest to the menu: the signature beef-tomato soup with diced potatoes. In recent years, the Hainan House's menu has been expanded to include Vietnamese as well as Chinese dishes.

ITALIAN CONNECTION

2725 TAYLOR STREET

Nestled in an area of Taylor Street more known for factories than fettucine, the Italian Connection can be easily bypassed. But that would be a regrettable mistake. *Courtesy* News-Sentinel.

The strip of Taylor Street is more associated with heavy industry than fine dining. That is part of what makes the Italian Connection one of Fort Wayne's best-kept secrets.

The intimate restaurant's two dining areas envelop you in atmosphere—far beyond the candlelit tables. Photographs of family and friends line the walls, and wine bottles line nearly every shelf and window sill. The music is midcentury classic (Frank Sinatra, Rosemary Clooney and the like).

Entree options, prepared under the supervision of thirty-five-year owner and head chef Alex Fiato, include homemade pastas and chicken, veal and seafood dishes.

OLEY'S

10910 U.S. 24 WEST

Oley is short for Olinger, the family with nearly forty years of pizza-baking experience. The original restaurant opened in Ossian in 1980 and eventually became known for its deep-dish, Chicago-style pies.

Their philosophy is spelled out on their homepage: "Oley's vow in 1980 was to bring to YOUR table the Purest, Finest, Freshest, and most 'Naturale' pizza pie in the business. That vow has not changed." Whether dropping by to pick up carryout or waiting to be seated in the dining room, patrons get to watch a little of the magic in action as Oley's employees choreograph the crust around their central pizza-making island, each adding their assigned contribution.

A second Oley's location, with much of the same great food but different ownership, has been operation at the corner of Lake Avenue and Coliseum Boulevard since 1993.

Oley's Pizza's southwest Fort Wayne location is a particularly popular spot before weekend football and basketball games, whether for dining in or carrying out. *Authors' collection.*

ORIENTAL GARDEN

120 WEST WASHINGTON BOULEVARD

A reminiscence by owner's son John Jung recalls Oriental Garden:

(It was) in the heart of downtown Fort Wayne, one block from the largest department store in town, Wolf & Dessauer's.

The restaurant was quite fancy for its day with a red and white glass front exterior, leather booths on both sides of the front half of the dining room, small "rooms" each containing a table and four chairs on both sides of the rear half of the dining room, and tables and chairs running the length down the middle of both halves. The dining room decoration included a pair of art deco planters shaped like modern pagodas.

We lived in a single-family home miles from downtown on the south side. The partners worked hard to allow their children to grow up as typical American kids in a suburban atmosphere.

Memories of his days at Harrison Hill Elementary School remained particularly vivid.

The Oriental Garden was one of only two Chinese restaurants in Fort Wayne at that time (there were also three Chinese laundries, Jung recalls). The kitchen boasted chefs versed in both Chinese and American cuisines (Jung's father was the Chinese chef); prime rib was a particular favorite. "I

Members of the Rochester (New York) Royals basketball team enjoy a meal at the Oriental Garden during a layover while playing the Fort Wayne Zollner Pistons. Chinese and American dishes were equally popular choices. *Courtesy* News-Sentinel.

remember firemen and policemen used to walk into the kitchen through the back door, spend a few minutes chatting with my dad and his partners over coffee, then walk out munching on prime rib sandwiches."

The Oriental Garden also was a favorite of the NBA's Rochester (New York) Royals, who dined there when in town to play the city's Zollner (later Detroit) Pistons. "And eat they did," Jung writes. "Huge T-bone steaks with all the trimmings, and drinking quarts of milk and orange juice by the bottle. I remember that even while seated at the tables gorging themselves, the players were so much taller than my dad and his partners who were walking around serving them."

PAGODA INN

6623 LINCOLN HIGHWAY EAST (APPROXIMATELY)

In August 1954, William Li was ready to open his second Chinese-American restaurant; his first was located on Lake Wawasee in Kosciusko County. He chose a site calculated to draw the attention of westbound Lincoln Highway travelers. A *News-Sentinel* article from the grand opening describes the Pagoda Inn's "decorative pieces which have been imported from China." It

adds, "The one-story restaurant… entrance leads into a lounge, beyond which lies the main dining room, which has a seating capacity of 110 persons." The article also notes that the Pagoda Inn was air-conditioned.

Top: William Li lived in a house behind his Pagoda Inn restaurant. The move made him heir to the chicken empire of William Holterman. *Courtesy Randy Harter.*

Bottom: Many businesses proclaim that "all roads lead to" wherever it is they are located. In the case of the Pagoda Inn, that just may have been true, if this postcard is any indication. *Courtesy Randy Harter.*

The Pagoda stood in the shadow of Li's other purchase, the "castle" that sat immediately to the west. Known as Holter's Roost, the fieldstone home sat at the center of William Holterman's chicken-breeding empire (among his other achievements, Holterman was a founder of Valparaiso University). Though the Pagoda is long gone, the home where the Holterman and Li families each once lived remains standing as the offices of the used-car lot that surrounds the building.

SAIGON RESTAURANT

2006 South Calhoun Street

The Saigon has been lauded by at least one reviewer for its "big-city vitality." "Vietnamese, Spanish and English words mingled into multicultural music," wrote Carol Tannehill of her visit. "Asian, Hispanic and Caucasian customers leaned over big soup bowls and sizzling stir-fries. Clinks and clangs rang from the kitchen."

For almost twenty-five years, Chinese dishes have augmented the menu of Vietnamese fare available at the Saigon Restaurant, south of downtown. *Authors' collection.*

Open since the summer of 1993, the Saigon was founded by the brother-and-sister pair of Tu Mai, who had been a pharmacy student, and Ve Phan, a chef. They were beckoned to the Midwest from San Jose, California, by a friend, Mai Hoang, who had previously run a restaurant in the same building.

The menu features Vietnamese soups and rice dishes that came with the siblings from their hometown of Long Xuyen. Cantonese, Mandarin and Szechuan meals are also available for those whose tastes tend more toward Chinese. And for diners unfamiliar with the ways of Vietnamese cuisine, servers are happy to demonstrate the proper way to best enjoy your meal.

THE VENICE

2242 GOSHEN ROAD

Before the construction of Coliseum Boulevard (originally called the Circumurban) in the late 1940s, Goshen Road was a primary gateway into Fort Wayne from the north and west. In 1948, the Key Dining Room opened on the north side of the Lincoln Highway in an area known as Key Heights, which also featured a motel and a bowling alley. Since 1955, that restaurant has been known as The Venice and has featured traditional Italian favorites.

Homemade Italian favorites and live music from acts like the Gregg Bender Band are specialties at The Venice. This easily overlooked gem is on the Lincoln Highway's road out of Fort Wayne on its way to South Bend. *Courtesy* News-Sentinel.

Three years after the conversion, local artist James McBride added a true Venetian touch by painting a mural along the restaurant's back wall. The scene features notable landmarks of Italy's "City of Canals," including its famed Rialto Bridge and St. Mark's Cathedral. The mural is complemented by homier family wedding photographs adorning other walls. (McBride's work has also been on display at the Halls-owned Takaoka of Japan restaurant in downtown Fort Wayne.)

Pat and Judy Finley have been owners since 1981. Their food reflects their homemade approach. Doughs and breads are all prepared on-site, as are tangy sauces and sausage. The buffet features entrees from pizza to baked mostaccioli to fettuccine Alfredo. Lasagna is another customer favorite.

Cuisine of other cultures takes center stage from time to time: notably German and Mexican. The Venice is also a change-of-pace destination for a St. Patrick's Day celebration.

ZOLI'S FAMILY RESTAURANT & LOUNGE

2426 BROADWAY

Zoltan Herman was a Fort Wayne fixture for more than four decades, but his remarkable story had its origins in Communist-era Hungary. A 1986 *News-Sentinel* profile of Herman tells it as so:

> *In 1956, the 23-year-old tool-and-die maker slipped across the Hungarian border into Austria during a Christmas Eve blizzard. He had no money, only the clothes on his back.*
>
> *Russian tanks had crushed the brief, bloody Hungarian uprising six weeks earlier, and Herman joined thousands of his countrymen fleeing*

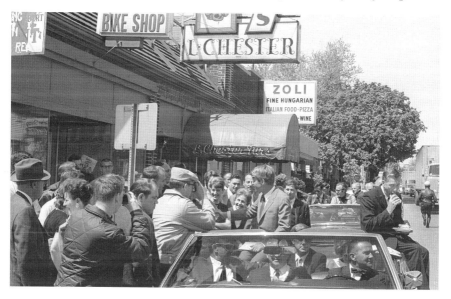

An unplanned stop by a major presidential candidate quickly drew a crowd along Broadway. A member of Bobby Kennedy's campaign entourage (out of the car at right) took advantage of the moment to grab a quick Zoli's ham sandwich. *Courtesy* News-Sentinel.

to the United States. But unlike many, who made a mad dash for the border, Herman chose the precise hour of his flight carefully. "I thought at Christmas time, the people have kindness and mercy. Even the Russian bears could give us a chance if they caught us."

Herman's odyssey led him to Fort Wayne, where a cousin was already living. Within five years, Herman had opened the restaurant that would occupy the rest of his life. But before opening Zoli's, he had worked as a floor mopper and dishwasher for Don Hall, Azar's and Johnelli's Pizza. There, owner John Spillson gave Herman his first job as a cook. When Spillson decided to convert Johnelli's into the more upscale Café Johnell, Herman struck out on his own, reasoning that the city was now in need of another pizza maker.

Herman's first restaurant experience had come working in his grandmother's place outside Budapest. He described his early years in Fort Wayne as a hand-to-mouth existence: "A friend gave me $100 to open up. We didn't even have a cash register. We put the money in a salad bowl under the bar. The first order was a stuffed pepper by the gas man."

Zoli's was a bakery as well as a full-service restaurant. Here, proprietor Zoltan Herman shows off some of the freshly baked goods. *Courtesy* News-Sentinel.

Over the years, Zoli's menu grew to include a variety of ethnic specialties in addition to the Hungarian cabbage rolls, gulyas, veal paprikash and those stuffed peppers. Herman ventured into Italian, Mexican, Greek, French and American cuisines. It was that pizza—and the exotic locale—that left its impression on one young patron.

Carol Tannehill recalled:

Back in the 1960s, my late father used to let me ride along when we'd pick up pizzas at Zoli's. That was back when pizza was a special treat, back when it was considered ethnic cuisine by diners in the Midwest. We'd walk into the steamy little carryout area and Zoli himself would be manning the kitchen. My father and I would look, wide-eyed, into the pastry case and marvel at the delicate cream horns, chocolate-iced eclairs, cherry-topped rum balls and nut-studded schnecken. We sniffed deeply to savor the scents of pungent cheeses, homemade sausages, goulash, cabbage rolls and beef stroganoff. And we talked to Zoli.

Herman's restaurant holdings grew to include Zoli's Hungry House (1969, sold in 1981) and Zoli's Chalet, later Zoli's Cowboy (1972, destroyed in a fire in 1986). But one of his singular memories remained the day Bobby Kennedy converted him to a Democrat—for one election anyway.

It was May 6, 1968, the day before Indiana's primary. The Kennedy campaign team hurriedly patronized Zoli's on its way to the airport after skipping a lavish fundraising lunch at the Keenan Hotel downtown. The motorcade stopped there on the request of Kennedy's wife, Ethel, who said she was famished.

As recounted in the *News-Sentinel* twenty-five years after the fact:

Zoli told his kitchen staff, which included his wife, Anna, to make a pizza and some ham-and-cheese sandwiches. The next thing he knew, his restaurant—then just a four-booth bar with a small family room in back—was swarming with Secret Service agents, the national media and any gawkers who could squeeze inside.

The two bonded as Kennedy asked Herman about tales of his escape from Hungary. Herman produced a special occasion bottle of Hungarian wine, and the two men drank toasts—Herman's: "To good luck and friendship." Kennedy's: "To the Hungarian freedom fighters."

Herman included a couple of souvenir menus with the party's takeout order. One was returned to him later that afternoon with Kennedy's signature and the inscription: "To Zoli: The best food I ever ate."

Kennedy won that Indiana primary, and four weeks later, he won the California primary. He was assassinated by Sirhan Sirhan on the night of June 6 in the kitchen of Los Angeles's Ambassador Hotel. Upon hearing the news, Herman purchased a wreath and placed it on the door of his restaurant.

Kennedy was far from the only politician to appreciate Herman's unique talents. Mayor Win Moses Jr. regularly held staff meetings in Zoli's back rooms, and Zoli's pizza was a frequent takeout go-to for helping people get through those long hours in the mayor's office—a trait Moses admired in the restaurateur. "I love Zoli's history, and I love his pastries," Moses said upon Herman's 2003 retirement. "He made it work by working 25 hours a day."

Herman died in December 2003 at age 70, months after failing health ushered him into that retirement. He never realized his dreams of returning to his native land and writing a cookbook. His four children had taken turns managing the restaurant so their father did not have to live in a world where Zoli's was no longer open. The Broadway location was later auctioned off, and the space was subdivided to house an aquatics supply store—and a pizzeria.

5
Fondly Remembered

BERGHOFF GARDENS

BERRY AND HARRISON STREETS

The Berghoff was a famed Chicago restaurant for a century; it was in Fort Wayne that the family and the business behind the name got their start.

The definitive authority, *The Berghoff Family Cookbook*, tells of how Herman Berghoff emigrated from Dortmund, Germany, at age seventeen. The highlight of his first several years of odd jobs was a year spent with Buffalo Bill's Wild West Show.

By 1874, Herman and younger brother Henry, who had arrived two years earlier, landed in the Summit City. In the year of America's centennial, Herman became a U.S. citizen. He continued to support himself with jobs as varied as jeweler and traveling salesman of shoes and boots. By 1883, Herman and Henry were operating the Berghoff Brothers East End Bottling Works, which eventually became the Herman Berghoff Brewing Co. The company, with its signature Dortmunder beer, was incorporated in April 1887.

Tragedy struck on August 22, 1888, when fire caused $50,000 in losses to Berghoff's brewery. As the family history tells it: "Herman was in his office while the fire raged overhead, writing telegrams to manufacturers about the damaged equipment, reordering new equipment, and asking for skilled workers to be sent post haste to install the new equipment." He was back

A starlit sky offered an ideal backdrop to the well-appointed Berghoff Gardens, the first instance of the now four-generation Spillson influence on the Fort Wayne food scene. *Courtesy Randy Harter.*

in business a month later. A second marriage in 1898, after the death of Herman's first wife, led to the family's move to Chicago.

A June 11, 1891, Fort Wayne newspaper advertisement for "Berghoff's Beer Garden" promised that "An elegant lunch will be served," with the namesake company's beer as a beverage option. By 1910, Fort Wayne, with a population of 63,000, was home to 197 saloons; 39 of them along Calhoun Street alone. And once the nation's experiment with Prohibition ended, Berghoff's was well-positioned to take advantage. An April 6, 1933, newspaper advertisement shows Nick Spillson holding the "much-coveted retail beer permit No. 1 for the city of Fort Wayne. A heavy business in beer is anticipated with its legal return here tonight," it adds. The business later passed into the hands of Charles Thotus.

In those post-Prohibition years, the Berghoff Gardens became known as a fine dining destination; it operated until 1957. Local historian Betty Stein reminisced of the Berghoff's glory days: "There was always a good live band

A postcard shows the well-stocked Berghoff Gardens bar, which was decked out in all its Art Deco glory. *Courtesy Randy Harter.*

playing and the food was excellent. Downstairs there was gambling, but that was a fairly well-kept secret and I didn't know about that until years later when it was closed down."

A set of period postcards touts the "beautiful" and "nationally famous" Berghoff Gardens as "famous for food" and "never closed."

The Berghoff name became prominent in connection with other products, including soap (that business eventually sold out to Procter & Gamble) and furnace burners. Henry Berghoff went on to become mayor of Fort Wayne; among his accomplishments was creation of the city's parks board. And along with brother Gustave, he helped found the German-American Bank. In the anti-German sentiment leading up to America's entrance into World War I, the bank was rechristened after the nation's sixteenth president. Lincoln Bank remained influential in the city for decades.

As for the Berghoff Gardens building, it housed a teen club for a several years after the restaurant closed. It was razed in 1964 after a suspected arson fire. The Berghoff brewery, which became part of the Falstaff line following a 1954 buyout, remained in operation until 1990.

CAPTAIN ALEXANDER'S WHARF

6200 COVINGTON PLAZA

This seafood-specialty restaurant operated on Fort Wayne's southwest side for twenty years. At the time of its 1994 closing, founder and namesake Alex Azar lamented, "Formal dining places all over the country are facing this problem. Years ago, no one would have thought of going into (the Wharf) without a tie. Now, nobody wears a tie in there." Azar declared the Wharf his "favorite place to eat."

A companion restaurant, the Moonraker, operated on Coliseum Boulevard at the site of what is now a Ruby Tuesday's. The restaurant's place mat explained the origin of the namesake word. "To the mariner, the

Top: "Captain Alexander" welcomed those hungry for seafood to the Wharf at the intersection of Jefferson Boulevard and Getz Roads, where a Walgreens now stands. *Courtesy* News-Sentinel.

Bottom: The Moonraker stood for years as a roadside architecture landmark at the intersection of Coliseum Boulevard and Parnell Avenue, near the Allen County War Memorial Coliseum. *Courtesy Randy Harter.*

sails of his ship were wings," it read. "It was the sails that gave life to a ship. The topmost sail was aptly referred to as the 'moonraker.' This uppermost wing of the ship would glide along the surface of the moon, challenging the heavens for its rightful position among the stars. Wives awaiting the return of their seagoing mates would view the moonraker first, and it signaled the time to prepare the day's or week's finest feast."

CARDINAL MUSIC PALACE

911 WEST WASHINGTON CENTER ROAD

"Five nights a week," recounted the *News-Sentinel*'s Barbara Wachtman, "the veteran organist (Bill Langford) tricks his listeners into believing he's creating an orchestra from four levels of keyboards, three octaves of foot pedals, all those pipes and a bunch of noise makers with his 10 short fingers that behave like acrobats on a keyboard.

"Langford curled his fingers as he took his hands off the keyboard. 'I used to despair greatly that I had these short fingers. But it's a matter of

At one end of the room in the Cardinal Music Palace sat the Mighty Wurlitzer organ. Pizza and pipes were popular attractions of the 1980s. *Courtesy* News-Sentinel.

gymnastics. And I have the extensions of my feet...after a while my feet just go on automatic pilot.' "

The object of Langford's affection was the Mighty Wurlitzer pipe organ. And the location was Fort Wayne's entry into the "pipes and pizza" restaurant trend that emerged in the early 1980s. About 5,000 diners a week turned out to hear the unique musical offerings of Langford and his fellow organist, Rick DeRose. Others to man the keyboard of the Mighty Wurlitzer included Buddy Nolan, Kirk Schakel, and Tom Wibbels.

The Wurlitzer came to the Summit City by way of Los Angeles. The 2,190-pipe instrument was originally installed in Grauman's Million Dollar Theatre, where it had provided the soundtrack for movies since the days of silent films. The zinc, copper, brass and wood pipes ranged in size from a half inch to thirty-two feet. Its instruments included a saxophone, trumpet, accordion, snare drum and tambourine. Other novelties of the organ, which rose out of the music palace's floor, included a trolley bell and a tugboat whistle. The organist was also in charge of the lighting effects throughout the room.

The two-story Cardinal Music Palace was built around the organ for $1.7 million (including the cost of acquiring the Mighty Wurlitzer). Renovations on the organ itself included thirty-plus coats of blue and gilt paint. Ken Crome, who installed the organ for the Cardinal Music Palace (he was also an investor), referred to the instrument as the "Cadillac of theater pipe organs. The Wurlitzers cut no corners and absolutely built the finest instrument you could build. And they got their price for it, so they didn't cut quality."

The organ was powered by a ten-horsepower turbine blower accompanied by a three-horsepower auxiliary blower. They combined to generate 1,000 cubic feet per minute of air.

In addition to pizza, the Cardinal featured a soda fountain. Its menu included pasta, sandwiches, a salad bar and soups.

The novelty eventually faded, and in September 1984, Cardinal Music Palace and its Mighty Wurlitzer went up for auction. Said auctioneer Dean Kruse, from Auburn: "I've sold zoos, I've sold a winery in the middle of Lake Erie and I've sold a railroad. But this has to be one of the most unusual things I've ever sold."

THE COLONIAL

NEW HAVEN AVENUE AT BEUTER ROAD

In the post–World War II years, the Colonial was a popular stop for either a quick bite or a full meal. It depended on which way you turned when you walked in the door. "The full service section was popular for leisurely Sunday family dinners while tourists and truckers appreciated counter and soda fountain service," recalls historian Nola G. Marquardt.

Frank Gardner (of Gardner's Sandwich Shop renown; he would also go on to found Fort Wayne's Char-King chain) appropriated the exterior design of the Howard Johnson's restaurants that were gaining popularity at the time. In addition to the two dining areas, a partial second story was the site of a banquet hall.

Soft ice cream brought many a diner to the Colonial. The restaurant was also known for its unique doughnut machine. According to Marquardt, the machine "resembled a small phone booth. Dough was made and put into the machine which shaped the donuts and dropped them into hot fat. The machine was enclosed with glass, allowing the cooking process to be viewed at all stages."

Marquardt also shared the story of an especially memorable Colonial employee:

There was…a fry cook by the name of Frank who had very irregular work habits. He often couldn't make it to work because of a "toothache," a malady which required quite a bit of whiskey to control. Tired of hearing the toothache excuse, Frank Gardner put him in the car and took him directly to see a dentist.

To readers of a certain age, the Howard Johnson influence (minus the garish aqua and orange accent color scheme) is obvious in the design of the Colonial. *Courtesy Randy Harter.*

Gardner opened the Colonial in late 1941. By 1946, he had sold the restaurant to Ora C. Baker. "Bake" had stepped in as manager during Gardner's military service. In 1954, the Colonial was taken over by J. Gail Myers and Charles A. Moore. Moore assumed full ownership in 1960 and operated the Colonial until its 1965 closing.

DEPOT CAFÉ

3500 NORTH WELLS STREET

A Southern Railroad dining car that seated forty-eight people was the main draw at the Depot Café. And the café was the centerpiece of the Wells Street Crossing Center business village, home to nearly forty shops. Established in 1976, the site also featured a 1926 Minnesota, Northfield & Southern Railway caboose, the office of developer Richard Ebnit. He had it redone in mahogany, accented with old Pullman car lighting fixtures.

When Ebnit bought the land, it comprised a farmhouse and four acres of fallow ground. His first year there, Ebnit devoted two of those acres to growing sweet corn and a third acre to pumpkins. "It was some of the best sweet corn I ever tasted," he told an interviewer. What did not sell, Ebnit roasted for friends at a giant on-site cookout. As the Crossing grew through the 1970s and 1980s, its tenants came to include a square dance apparel outfitter, a credit union and a dress designer. The site's collection of artifacts came to include the cupola of Fort Wayne's old Concordia High School.

Entrance to the café's dining car was through a depot building, which also had counter and table seating, as well as an assortment of railroad memorabilia. Also behind the counter was the former G.C. Murphy's

As an anchor of his Wells Street Crossing development, Richard Ebnit's Depot Café had a fairly short lifespan. But it rapidly developed a loyal clientele. *Courtesy* News-Sentinel.

doughnut machine, which Ebnit acquired after the five-and-dime store closed in 1985. (He also received recipes and the names of some of Murphy's ingredient suppliers.)

The Depot Café eventually gave way to another Fort Wayne favorite. In 1996, Ebnit sold his land to the next-door Edy's Grand Ice Cream plant, which wanted to add a cold storage warehouse.

THE EMBERS

505 EAST COLISEUM BOULEVARD

The Embers was a four-hundred-seat attachment to the Van Orman Northcrest Highway Hotel. It billed itself as "Mid-America's finest supper club, where you could (s)ee your steak prepared over hickory charcoal embers." Another advertising postcard boasted of the club's "Top name entertainment—Floor Shows nightly."

Entertainers could be found among the Embers' patrons as well. Veteran waitress Margaret Schuller came to the Embers following jobs at the 412 Club and the soda fountain at G.C. Murphy's. In a 1991 feature, Schuller recalled the evening she was selected to serve the visiting Rock Hudson and Marilyn Maxwell (who had grown up in Fort Wayne).

"The managers wanted them to get the best service, so they asked me to wait on them," Schuller recalled. "There was no ballyhoo—because that's the way they wanted it. No one even knew they were there."

Top: The Van Orman Northcrest was one of several incarnations of the hotel that was home to the Embers nightclub. *Courtesy Randy Harter.*

Bottom: Big-name stars were a common sight at the Embers—both onstage and, occasionally, in the audience. *Courtesy Randy Harter.*

In later years, the location at the northeast corner of Coliseum Boulevard and Coldwater Road was home to a succession of nightspots: the Sands, Gentry's and Rumors. The hotel also had changed hands; it became the Coliseum Motor Inn. The buildings finally succumbed to the wrecking ball in 1989 but not before revealing one final surprise.

While doing inventory on the inn's contents ahead of an auction, workers came across a pair of waterlogged boxes in the basement. Their contents proved to be a treasure trove of information on performers from the supper club's Sands incarnation. The clippings, publicity photographs and other memorabilia detailed appearances by the Tommy Dorsey Orchestra, Louis Jordan and his Tympany Five, the Crosby kids (Bing's sons Dennis, Lindsay and Phil) and famed drummers Buddy Rich and Gene Krupa, as well as a host of other entertainers.

FAMILY & FRIENDS CAFÉ

5830 WEST JEFFERSON BOULEVARD

Carol Galbraith and her daughter Belinda Plank kept alive the memory of Fort Wayne's legendary Hobby House in a restaurant that was uniquely their own. One writer referred to Family & Friends as the kind of place that "provided plenty of warm fuzzies to world-weary homebodies."

Galbraith was the daughter of Hobby House proprietor Phil Clauss. Some of the recipes at Family & Friends were those of her late father. Other comfort-food staples available at the cafeteria-style restaurant included sandwiches, salads, soups and home-style desserts.

For about a decade, from the spring of 1995 to the fall of 2004, Family & Friends was a Time Corners staple. After Galbraith and Plank stepped aside, citing burnout, health issues and a lack of staff, chef Chris Redden took over for a time.

Family & Friends Cafe: A Collection of our Favorite Recipes. Authors' collection.

A cookbook written by the mother and daughter in 2001 lays out on the back cover their simple mission: "Carol and Belinda love to cook. They believed in a spiritual connection to their father/grandfather and that their love for people creates a perfect place for them to share their love of great food. It's the spiritual connection, love of family & friends, good food, warmth and comfort that is special here."

The cookbook, like the restaurant, was a tribute to Phil Clauss: "He started the dream and we have carried it on. We know he is proud of our efforts and feel that the circle is complete. We are grateful that we could share in it."

G.C. MURPHY CO.

823 South Calhoun Street

Like many downtown department stores of its day, Murphy's was a place where you could get a quick, cheap lunch. For at least one Fort Wayne businessman, it was also a barometer of the economy.

"I used to measure inflation by their one-on-one breakfasts," said Donnelly P. McDonald, chairman and president of Summcorp, the holding company for Summit Bank. "In 1962, one piece of bacon, one piece of toast, an egg and coffee cost 29 cents," he said in 1985. "Today it's $1.49." Cake doughnuts were another well-loved breakfast item. The machine that made them continues in operation today just a few blocks away, at Cindy's Diner.

The lunch counter was a staple of the Murphy's experience. As the G.C. Murphy Company Foundation website puts it: "Before there were 'fast-food'

Another business that sat in the shadow of Indiana's once-tallest building, G.C. Murphy was at the intersection of Calhoun and Wayne Streets. *Courtesy News-Sentinel.*

The dining counter at G.C. Murphy was typical of lunch counters at many department stores of the day. Shoppers merely had to step across the aisle to sit down at one of the stools for a break and a meal or snack. *Courtesy ARCH.*

chains, Murphy's lunch counters in cities large and small united rich and poor, men and women, who needed a quick, cheap and filling 'bite to eat' before returning to the office or factory."

Food was just part of the attraction of the store that was a downtown fixture between February 4, 1928, and January 1, 1986 (the restaurant was shuttered on October 23, 1985). The 225,000-square-foot building that housed Murphy's for its final thirty-five years opened at a cost of $1.75 million in 1950. At its peak, Murphy's employed about four hundred people. By the end, that number had dwindled to about sixty. A $150,000 spruce-up in the early 1980s was not enough to save the Ames Department store affiliate. (A Southtown Mall location had closed in 1979.)

As then mayor Win Moses Jr. saw it, the last of the downtown department stores "was almost in a time warp. When I saw the movie 'Back to the Future,' the first thing I thought about was Murphy's. Times changed, but it didn't."

HILGER'S FARM RESTAURANT
13210 U.S. 30 WEST

"We educated many, many teenagers to the workforce," John Hilger once said of his family's distinctive barn-shaped restaurant. A fair number of those employees dated one another; some even married. "We were better at that than serving food," Hilger modestly joked.

The family's story begins in 1925, when Henry Hilger took his horse-drawn carriage door-to-door in Fort Wayne to offer customers the onions and carrots grown on the family farm on the Lincoln Highway west of town. (Henry eventually upgraded to a Model T). In 1973, sons John and Joe Hilger decided to have the public come to them instead; they opened a farm market that featured the same Hilger-grown produce, plus locally made baked goods and cheeses. According to Henry Hilger's *News-Sentinel* obituary: "The farm market began with peas and corn. Eventually, several other vegetables and strawberries were added, and Hilger's became a popular 'pick-your-own' site."

In 1987, the Hilgers expanded further by opening the restaurant. At its peak, Hilger's employed up to 350 people, many of them teenagers in their first job.

Among Hilger's specialties was its mashed potatoes; they were loaded with cream, butter, garlic, salt and pepper. "We're one of the biggest potato growers in the state," John said. It was estimated that Hilger's employees peeled between 2,000 and 3,000 pounds of potatoes weekly. But as John's mom, Sally, said, those potatoes were the exception when it came to food preparation at Hilger's. "Most of our food takes very little extra flavoring," she said in an interview. "We take most of (the farm produce) right from the ground and serve it. You get more vitamins and flavor if you don't cook it so much. Vine-ripened food is the best."

For John, his satisfaction came from seeing his customers satisfied. "I enjoy watching people enjoy what you put in front of them," he said.

Hilger's Farm Restaurant featured a second-floor banquet hall and became a popular site for company picnics. The picturesque setting was also the launching spot for campaigns by a number of Hoosier politicians, with Richard Lugar, Dan Quayle and Dan Coats among them. Others who gave the restaurant their thumb's up included President Ronald Reagan and radio personality Paul Harvey.

At harvest time, Hilger's Fall Pumpkin Festival drew families to attractions that included hayrides, a straw maze and pyramid and plenty of rides.

The restaurant closed in 2006, but produce still is available at a family farm stand just off U.S. 30 as well as in the pick-your-own fields. John Hilger, who served as a board member for Northwest Allen County Schools and was active with Fort Wayne's Community Harvest Food Bank, passed away in April 2017 while vacationing in Amsterdam.

HOBBY HOUSE

230 EAST WAYNE STREET

Hobby House is notable for its connection to a pair of fast-food giants. It is where Fort Wayne was introduced to the eleven herbs and spices of Kentucky Fried Chicken, and it is where the founder of Wendy's got his start.

Phil Clauss opened the Hobby House in 1948; His 155-seat restaurant served breakfast and lunch every day but Saturday. Over the front door, the Hobby House advertised "popular foods at popular prices."

Among Clauss's employees was a fifteen-year-old Dave Thomas, whose adoptive family had made the trek north from Knoxville, Tennessee. Thomas elected to stay even as the family prepared to move again. He dropped out of school to support himself, and he did not obtain his GED until 1993. Thomas considered the decision to leave school the worst of his life, and it turned him into an advocate for education—in addition to adoption—causes.

As Clauss took note of Thomas's diligence in even the most routine tasks, like busing tables and washing dishes, Thomas rose through the ranks. Clauss eventually made Thomas manager of the Hobby House Ranch Restaurant at North Anthony Boulevard and Crescent Avenue.

In this photograph, the Hobby House advertises its "popular food at popular prices." It also prominently features advertising for Colonel Sanders's "internationally famous" Kentucky Fried Chicken. *Courtesy Randy Harter.*

Outside the Hobby House on April 9, 1954, the Al Tansor World Championship Rodeo arrived. Cowboy star Kenne Duncan, left, was billed as "the meanest man in the movies"; he was accompanied by western singer Ruthie Mack, who did double duty as the target holder for Duncan's sharpshooting act. Six-year-old Terry Haver, of Hicksville, Ohio, is the lucky young cowboy. *Courtesy* News-Sentinel.

In a you-can't-make-this-stuff-up twist, the Hobby Ranch site is now home to a Wendy's restaurant. Thomas visited that store—the 5,300th in the Wendy's chain—in 1998.

"Yep. It all started right here," he reminisced to a newspaper interviewer during that stop. "I used to live around the corner and this is also where the Colonel (Sanders) walked in and eventually became one of my mentors.

"I have so many fond memories about this place," Thomas added. "It was here that I worked a lot of hours and met people who gave me a real good start in this business."

Thomas remained on the Colonel's radar when in 1962 he accepted Clauss's offer to take over four of Clauss's KFC franchises that were floundering in Columbus, Ohio. Thomas was promised a 45 percent stake if he was able to turn the stores around. His success was evident when he and a partner sold those stores back to KFC for $1.5 million in 1968. Thomas opened his first Wendy's in Columbus a year later.

Wendy's grew to become the world's third-largest hamburger chain. Legend has it that the signature square hamburgers got their shape as Thomas kept in mind the advice of his grandmother: "Don't cut corners." And Thomas became a television commercial staple through the late 1980s and 1990s as the folksy pitchman for the restaurants named for one of his daughters. He was estimated to have filmed more than eight hundred spots, a record for a company-founder/pitchman. In a previous Wendy's advertisement campaign, Clara Peller introduced America to the well-remembered catchphrase, "Where's the beef?"

A former Hobby House patron shared her own insight into Thomas during his 1998 visit to his old stomping grounds.

"The thing I most admire about him is that he still remembers who we are," said Lorraine Shubert. "We've never been in one place together where he didn't recognize us. He's just a wonderful guy."

As for the Hobby House, its flagship downtown restaurant closed in August 1999. Its owners cited a recently enacted city ordinance that banned smoking in restaurants, which they said led to an almost immediate 20 percent drop in business. Phil Clauss's daughter Carol continued her father's restaurant tradition. After working at the Hobby House for years, she went on to open the Family & Friends Café in Time Corners.

MARGY'S CAFÉ

VARIOUS LOCATIONS

Before striking out on her own, Margy Hooker was a caterer and the food and beverage director for Fort Wayne's renowned Sycamore Hills Golf Club. She put her own vision in place when she opened her café in the Covington Plaza shopping center in March 1996.

As described by the *News-Sentinel*, Hooker's vision was of a "sunny new breakfast-and-lunch cafe with salmon pink walls and fresh California cuisine."

"I think everybody's excited to have something new and different opening out here," she said of her southwest-side location (which had formerly been

Left: *Margy's Favorite Recipes. Authors' collection.*

Right: Margy Hooker's face became a familiar one to those in search of fresh, light, California-style fare—with a big emphasis on fruit. *Courtesy* News-Sentinel.

home to Frederico's Italian restaurant). "We needed something like this for the community, I think."

In keeping with the California fresh theme, fruit factored heavily into Margy's décor and logo, which featured a pair of black raspberries. The floor tiles—all eight tons—were hand-painted in Mexico and had accents of raspberries, bananas, kiwis, apples, plums, oranges, strawberries and cherries. That accenting carried through to the curtains and chairs as well. (There were seats for one hundred, plus ten more at the coffee and juice bar.) The coffee Margy's served had been grown at the bottom of a Guatemalan volcano; roasting was saved for post-harvest from the depths.

Nearly four years to the month, the Covington Plaza location abruptly closed in February 2000, the casualty of a legal dispute that had also claimed the nearby Alumni Club (of which Hooker was also a co-owner). But she quickly found a new venue, joining the Ribbons & Herbs Tea Room and Specialty Gift Shop in Leo. That business, which expanded by

1,200 square feet to accommodate Hooker's patrons, had been opened by her longtime friends and former Margy's employees Sandra Miller and Patty Middaugh. That venture lasted about a year.

Hooker's next project was her locally published cookbook, *Margy's Favorite Recipes*. The book features 330 dishes that spanned her career. And with a cookbook collection that had grown to nearly 400 over 30 years, Hooker had specific ideas for her book on everything from layout to binding. She said the book was a thank-you to her many fans. "It's nice to know the restaurant meant so much to people," she told an interviewer. "I've even had people call me with (potential new restaurant locations): 'You could reopen Margy's there, couldn't you?'"

By late 2004, Hooker was ready to try again. Margy's Café reopened inside Latitudes, a Dupont Road complex that featured home décor, floral, and artisan shops, plus other independent vendors. The new Margy's featured fewer menu options than its southwest-side forerunner but had much of the same ambience in a more deli-like setting that even accommodated a drive-up window. "The cafe is bright and festive," reported reviewer Carol Tannehill, "with metal-and-glass garden-style furniture, an openwork gazebo and lots of windows bringing the outdoor feeling inside." That attention to detail extended to the food presentation, with Tannehill praising Margy's "pretty plates. Fresh berries, ruffled lettuce and other edible garnishes were artsy, thoughtful touches."

The final location lasted about a year and a half, closing in March 2006. "I am so grateful to our loyal customers," Hooker said as Margy's closed for the final time. "We've grown very close through the years. Their support and genuine kindness touched us."

MILLER'S TEA ROOM

Harrison Street and Jefferson Boulevard

Miller's was located at the site of the current Courtyard by Marriott hotel. Luella Miller was proprietress of an establishment that was known variously as Miller's English Tea Room, English Terrace Restaurant and the Terrace Room Restaurant and Cocktail Lounge (in the 1950s). For a time, the building's second floor was home to the Colonial Hotel.

Historian Betty Stein remembers the English Terrace as a popular restaurant where "often there was a pianist who played requests and supplied

This always elegantly appointed restaurant went through a number of incarnations through its existence; here, it is seen in postcard form as Miller's Tea Room and in a pair of photographs as the English Terrace. *Courtesy Randy Harter.*

The Terrace Room Restaurant & Cocktail Lounge was likely a popular stop for guests at the Indiana Hotel across Harrison Street along Jefferson Boulevard. *Courtesy* News-Sentinel.

'atmosphere.' " And a 1954 postcard touts the Terrace as "specializing in fine steaks, chops, fresh sea food and excellent cocktails," also noting that the restaurant is "recommended by Duncan Hines."

PAPA SUZETTI'S

3509 NORTH CLINTON STREET

In a city where everyone who aspires to serve Italian cuisine must face comparison to the Casa restaurants, Bob Westerhausen was able to make a name for himself, as Papa Suzetti.

"It's a family operation," Westerhausen told an interviewer in 1984. "I probably see more of my family than most." Westerhausen's wife, three daughters and son all had roles in the restaurant. He estimated his workday lasted from 9:00 a.m. to 2:00 a.m., seven days a week.

Westerhausen studied accounting after graduating from North Side High School. He bought what was then called the Spaghetti Bowl as an investment in 1978. "But, it wasn't long until he was totally involved, not only in administration and management, but in the kitchen, creating new dishes for the Italian menu," the newspaper profile reported.

Though the restaurant is long closed, the tastes of Papa Suzetti's can still be had; it just takes a little more work. In 1994, Sharon Westerhausen published the cookbook *Recreate Papa Suzetti's Memories.*

Recreate Papa Suzetti's Memories. Authors' collection.

WINDOW GARDEN CAFÉ

ONE SUMMIT SQUARE

The Window Garden Café featured spectacular views of the city from its location on the thirteenth floor of One Summit Square. The cafeteria, which served breakfast and lunch from 1982 to 2014, was open to the public but mostly served workers inside the building.

WOLF & DESSAUER

923–931 SOUTH CALHOUN STREET

Back in the days when the department store was the hub of every city's downtown, Wolf & Dessauer was Fort Wayne's place to be...and be seen. And one of the highlights of a Wolf & Dessauer visit was lunch at the sixth-floor tearoom. A June 1921 newspaper advertisement boasted of the tearoom's "snowy white linen and silverware, glistening with cleanliness." The advertisement also promised "no annoying delays. SERVICE INSTANTANEOUS. You get just what you want and you get it immediately." By June 1940, the menu for the Wolf & Dessauer Tea Room and Men's Grill boasted that the rooms were "Air Conditioned for Your Comfort."

An additional feature of the ladies-only tearoom was the models who walked through, showing off the fashions available elsewhere in the store.

Wolf & Dessauer was a destination for more than its tearoom and lunch counter. Its lighted Santa display has been refurbished and continues to delight Christmas revelers nearly eighty years after its 1940 debut. *Courtesy* News-Sentinel.

Among the specialties on the menu crafted by tearoom manager Edith Goodyear was frozen fruit salad. "It was to die for," recalls Fort Wayne historian Betty Stein, a Wolf & Dessauer employee in the 1930s and 1940s. "That's what the women ordered."

For others, the basement fountain room sufficed. In her *News-Sentinel* By the Way column, Stein reported the reminiscences of Donna Peebles. "I loved sitting up in at the counter on those tall stools," Peebles said. "And the best thing on the menu was a cashew nut butter sandwich. Now, peanut butter is great, but cashew nut butter is heavenly, and that was the only place I knew of in town where one could get it." Stein added that Peebles's "goal was not to let any of that runny filling get away, although she knew she mustn't lick her fingers."

Selected Bibliography

Berghoff, Carlyn, Jan Berghoff, and Nancy Ross Ryan. *The Berghoff Family Cookbook*. Kansas City, MO: Andrews McMeel Publishing, 2007.

Duffy, Reid. *Reid Duffy's Guide to Indiana's Favorite Restaurants*. Bloomington, IN: Quarry Books, 2006.

Elchert, Keith, and Laura Weston-Elchert. *Honest Eats: Celebrating the Rich Food Heritage of Indiana's Historic Lincoln Highway*. Evansville, IN: MT Publishing, 2016.

Harter, Randolph L. *Fort Wayne*. Charleston, SC: Arcadia Publishing, 2013.

Harter, Randolph L., and Craig S. Leonard. *Legendary Locals of Fort Wayne*. Charleston, SC: Arcadia Publishing. 2015.

Jung, John. *Sweet and Sour: Life in Chinese Family Restaurants*. N.p.: Yin & Yang Press, 2011.

Lupke, David B. "The History of Fort Wayne's Bars and Taverns: From the Jesuits to World War II." Presentation to the Fort Wayne Quest Club. October 2, 2015.

Marquardt, Nola G. "The Colonial Restaurant." *Old Fort News*, Vol. 67, no. 2. 2004.

————. "Gardner's Drive-in Sandwich Stand." *Old Fort News*, Vol. 67, no. 2. 2004.

Patrick, Rebecca. "Embracing the History: Allen County Business Legacies Live On." *BizVoice*/Indiana Chamber. January/February 2017.

Violette, Ralph. *Fort Wayne, Indiana*. Charleston, SC: Arcadia Publishing, 1999.

Wiehe, Jeff. "Still Got It." *Fort Wayne*. June 2017.

Index

A

Adams, Mike 10
Anderson, John "Pat,"
    Myra, Wes 24
Atz, Frank 33
Atz's Ice Cream Shoppe 33
Avery, Jane 36
Azar, Alexander 35, 86
Azar, David 35
Azar, George 36, 43
Azar's 34, 35, 36, 43, 80

B

Back 40 Junction 35
Baker, Ora C. 90
Baldus, Patricia 54
Bandido's 66
Bankert, Joe 27
Bearcreek Farm 28
Bearcreek Memories Dinner
    Theater 28
Beatty, John D. 22
Berghoff Gardens 68, 70,
    84, 85
Berghoff, Gustave 85
Berghoff, Henry 83

Berghoff, Herman 83
Billings, Matt 14
Billy's Downtown Zulu 10
Bixby, Dan, Jeanne 27
Blackie's Corral Rib Bar 67
Bob's 11
Brand-Beere, Cathy 56
Brand, Tim 56
Bridgewater Golf Club 58
Brown, Paula 60

C

Cafe Johnell 68, 70, 80
Captain Alexander's Wharf
    86
Cardinal Music Palace 88
Carney, Bob 10
Cartwright, Lester 31
Casaburo, Tom 71
Casa D'Angelo 71
Casagrande, Frank 60
Centlivre, Charles L. 17
Chappell, Gary 53
Chappell's Coral Grille 52
Char-King 43, 89
Chester, Lucille 20
Chien Tran 72

Choka, Kathy 38
Choka, Russ 38
Chop's 32
Clauss, Phil 92, 93, 96, 98
Clevenger, Rob, Stacy 32
Club Soda 32, 53, 54
Coats, Dan 95
Colchin, Neil 12
Colonial, The 89, 90, 105
Community Harvest Food
    Bank 36, 96
Coney Island 38, 39
Connett, Don 17
Cork 'N Cleaver 54
Country Kitchen 56
Cozmas, Nicholas 9
Crome, Ken 88

D

D'Angelo, Jim 71
D'Angelo, Jimmy 21
Dash-in Cafe 12
Dawson's 39, 40
Dawson, Virginia 39
DeBrand Chocolates 56
Deli 620 61
Del-Mar Bar 61

Depot Cafe 37, 60, 90, 91
DeRose, Rick 88
Diem Huynh 72
Diettrich, Sebastian 51
Don Hall 16, 80
Dorikis, Harry 38
Downs, Pamela 57
Duffy, Reid 44, 58, 59, 61, 105
Durnell, Denny, Teena 13

E

Ebnit, Richard 90
Eddie Merlot's 55
Embers, The 91
Empyrean Events and Catering 65
English Terrace Restaurant 100
Eschoff, Vasil 38
Evelyn Robbins Restaurant 27

F

Family & Friends Cafe 92
Fiato, Alex 74
Fiechter, Julia 65
Filippou, Christina 63
Filippou, Von 61
Fort Wayne Komets 57
Fort Wayne Zollner Pistons 31, 76
412 Club 91
Frappier, Christian 70
Frederico's Italian restaurant 99
Freeland, Dick 8
Freistroffer, Hank 66
Funk, Peg 23

G

Galbraith, Carol 92
Gard, Brenda, Steve 59

Gardner, Francis W. 40, 43, 89
Gardner's 7, 40, 42, 43, 89, 105
Gary Probst 65
G.C. Murphy's 37, 90, 91, 93
Gentry's 92
Germania Grill 70
Goodyear, Edith 104
Gounaris, Petros 63
Grantham, Todd 46
Green Frog 13
Grinsfelder, Alan 54

H

Hadley, Robert 31
Hainan House 72
Hall, Bud 16, 17
Hall, Don 14
Hall, Jeff 16
Hall, Michael 48
Hall's 16, 17, 71
Hall, Sam 17
Hammerle Tavern 27
Harlan House Cafe 43
Harter, Angie 37
Hartley's 57, 58
Haystack Inn 10
Heinecke, Evelyn, Gerhard 43
Helmke, Paul 42, 64
Helmke, Walter E. 42
Henry, Chris, Kurt, Matt 61
Henry, Cindy 13
Henry, Lou 25, 63
Henry's 18
Herman, Zoltan 79
Hilger, Henry 95
Hilger, Joe 95
Hilger, John 95
Hilger's Farm Restaurant 95
Hobby House 32, 42, 92, 96, 98
Holmes, John 22
Holterman, William 77

Home Lunch 27
Hooker, Margy 98
Hoosier Tavern 58
Hubartt, Kerry 8
Humbrecht, Greg 19
Humbrecht, Jack 19, 20
Humphries, William 55

I

Italian Connection 73

J

Jack & Johnny's 19
Jacquay, Greg 28
Jainagerker, Rajib 38
Jimmie's Pizza 66
Joe's Tap Tavern 27
Johnelli's Pizza 68, 80
Johnston, Hughie 58

K

Karn, John 22
Kennedy, Bobby 81
Kentucky Fried Chicken 96
Key Dining Room 78
Klemm, Mike 20
Klemm's Candlelight Cafe 20
Kneubuhler, Dan 23
Knoblauch, Jeff, Mary 50
Kruse, Dean 88

L

La Margarita 68
Langford, Bill 87
Larson, Cindy 8, 22, 25
Laycoff, Alexandria, Lazar 20
Laycoff, Barbara, Cyril 20
Laycoff-Richards, Angie 20
Lazoff, Thomas 20
Liberty Diner 43, 44
Lindi's 61

Lindi's Gourmet Market and Deli 60
Li, William 76
L&L Tavern 20
Lodge at Coyote Creek 25
Lombard, Carole 53
Long, Shelley 13
Lugar, Richard 95
Lunch Box Cafe 43
Lupke, David 59
Lupke, David B. 27

M

Mad Anthony Brewpub and Eatery 46
Mai Hoang 78
Margy's Cafe 99
Marquardt, Nola G. 40, 89
Marriott's Red River Steaks and BBQ 35
Maxwell, Marilyn 91
McBride, James 78
McDonald, Donnelly P. 93
McLeod, Hartley Jr., Sue 57, 58
McLeod, Hartley Sr., Wanda 57
Melchi, Mark 46
Messman, Karon 63
Middaugh, Patty 100
Miller, Lindi 60
Miller, Luella 100
Miller, Sandra 100
Miller's Tea Room 100
Mills, Christina 19
Moonraker 86
Moore, Charles A. 90
Morton, Alice 13
Moses, Win Jr. 81, 94
Motz, George 48
Munchie Emporium 46
Myers, J. Gail 90

N

Nei, Mark 25, 27
Nessman, Billy 11
Nick's Martini Bar 16
Nine Mile Restaurant 22
Nolan, Buddy 88

O

Ochoa, Panfilo 67
Ochoa, Pantaleon 67
Oetting, Ferdinand 59
07 Pub 70
Olde Towne Diner 23
Old Mill Grill and Bar 70
Oley's 74
Oriental Garden 74, 75, 76
O'Sullivans Italian Pub 60
Oyster Bar 58, 59

P

Pagoda Inn 76
Palm Gardens 29
Papas, Stilos 38
Papa Suzetti's 103
Parrish, Amy, Jeff 10
Paula's On Main 59
Pence, Greg 19
Pence, Johnny 19
Penick, Marilyn 48
Peters, Ott 53
Pflueger, Teresa 44
Pio, Carlyle 16
Plank, Belinda Belinda 92
Podzielinski, Lynn 12
Powers, Esther Leo 23, 47, 48
Powers Hamburgers 7, 47, 48
Powers, Rolin 48
Puritan Ice Cream 33

Q

Quayle, Dan 64, 95

R

Rack & Helen's 24
Redden, Chris 92
Redwood Inn Redwood 25
Rekeweg, Erwin "Rack," Helen 24
Ribbons & Herbs Tea Room and Specialty Gift Shop 99
Rib Room 16, 61, 63
Richards 27, 28
Roach, Danny 44
Rumors 92

S

Saigon 77, 78
Samaras, James 38
Sanders, Col. Harlan 97
Sands, The 92
Schakel, Kirk 88
Scheele, Cindy, John 36
Schindler, Jimmy 66
Schindler, Jimmy II 66
Schnee, Joseph 59
Schuller, Margaret 91
Seyfert, Daniel 54
Shopoff's 30
Smith, Jason 53
Smitty's Tasty Burger Shop 49
Smyrniotis, George 43
Sokolik, Tom 60
Spaghetti Bowl 102
Spillson, John 68, 80
Spillson, Jon 70
Spillson, Marcus 70, 71
Spillson, Nicholas 68, 84
Spillson, Nike 70
Stamanis, Nick 61
Statler, Vicki 44
Stein, Betty 42, 84, 100, 104
Stewart, Wes 27
Stine, Ilene (Roach) 44
Strauss, A.M. 71

Strong, Don 27
Strong, Gladys 27
Stuckey, Blaine 46
Sullivan, Jimmy 21
Summers, Neal 31, 60
Summit Club 64, 65, 70
Sweet Lou's Pizza 63

T

Tannehill, Carol 7, 24, 27,
    34, 46, 48, 72, 77,
    80, 100
Tapp, Mike 9
Ted Gouloff's Paramount
    Grill 72
Terrace Room Restaurant
    and Cocktail
    Lounge 100
Thomas, Dave 42, 96
TJ's Pasta 72
Trion Tavern 28
Trolley Bar 18, 29, 31,
    32, 60
Trump, Donald 57
Tu Mai 78

V

Van Orman Northcrest
    Highway Hotel 91
Venice 78, 79
Ve Phan 78

W

Wendy's 42, 96, 97, 98
Westerhausen, Bob 102
Westerhausen, Sharon 103
Whippy Dip 48, 50
Wibbels, Tom 88
Wilson, Jerry 70
Witcher, Jeff 19
Wolf & Dessauer 74, 103,
    104

Y

Yacht Club 57
Young, Don 32, 60

Z

Zesto's 50, 51
Zoli's 80, 81, 82

About the Authors

Laura Weston was previously the book editor at Fort Wayne Newspapers and the former multimedia editor for the *News-Sentinel* in Fort Wayne, Indiana. She is a native of Marion, Ohio, and a graduate of Westfield-Washington (Indiana) High School. She holds a bachelor's degree in American history from Ball State University and studied historic preservation and urban planning in graduate school there. She served as past president of the board of the Indiana Lincoln Highway Association during the highway's centennial year in 2013. She currently serves on the board of the Allen County Friends of the Parks and is member of the Fort Wayne History Roundtable.

Keith Elchert is copy editor of the editorial pages for the *Journal Gazette* in Fort Wayne, Indiana. He is a native of Tiffin, Ohio, and a graduate of Tiffin Columbian High School. He has a bachelor's degree in communication from the University of Dayton and a master's degree in journalism from Ball State University. He has served as president of the Indiana Lincoln Highway Association.

The two have collaborated on two previous books: *Tiffin* (Arcadia Publishing, 2014) and *Honest Eats: Celebrating the Rich Food History of Indiana's Historic Lincoln Highway* (MT Publishing, 2016).

Visit us at
www.historypress.com